冶金工业出版社

普通高等教育“十四五”规划教材

Practical Crew Resource Management Course Manual for Student Pilots

飞行学员机组资源管理实用教程

杜丽娟　编著

扫一扫查看全书
数字资源

北　京
冶　金　工　业　出　版　社
2022

Introduction
内容简介

The book is divided into 6 units with 15 lessons in total. Each unit is comprised of lead-in, case analysis, training briefing. The book covers 6 aspects: introduction to crew resource management, crew communication, situational awareness, pilot judgment and aeronautical decision making, cockpit leadership and cockpit automation.

This book is not only suitable for students majoring in flight technology, air traffic control and flight dispatch in colleges and universities, but also for relevant staff of aviation enterprises and institutions, Civil Aviation Administration and its subordinate administrations. At the same time, it can also be used as a self-learning reference for flight enthusiasts.

本书分为6篇，共15课，每篇都配有课文导读、案例分析、训练讲评等内容。书中内容涉及机组资源管理概论、机组沟通与交流、情景意识、判断与决策、驾驶舱领导、驾驶舱自动化6个方面。

本书不仅适合高等院校飞行技术、空中交通管制、飞行签派专业的学生使用，也可供航空企事业单位、民航局及其下属管理局的相关工作人员作为培训教材使用，同时也可作为飞行爱好者的自学参考书。

图书在版编目(CIP)数据

飞行学员机组资源管理实用教程 = Practical Crew Resource Management Course Manual for Student Pilots：汉文、英文/杜丽娟编著. —北京：冶金工业出版社，2022.5

普通高等教育“十四五”规划教材

ISBN 978-7-5024-9124-6

Ⅰ.①飞…　Ⅱ.①杜…　Ⅲ.①航空运输管理—高等学校—教材—汉、英　Ⅳ.①F560.8

中国版本图书馆CIP数据核字（2022）第062073号

Practical Crew Resource Management Course Manual for Student Pilots
飞行学员机组资源管理实用教程

出版发行　冶金工业出版社　　电　话　(010)64027926
地　址　北京市东城区嵩祝院北巷39号　　邮　编　100009
网　址　www.mip1953.com　　电子信箱　service@mip1953.com

责任编辑　王　颖　美术编辑　彭子赫　版式设计　郑小利
责任校对　李　娜　责任印制　禹　蕊
北京虎彩文化传播有限公司印刷
2022年5月第1版，2022年5月第1次印刷
787mm×1092mm　1/16；9.5印张；225千字；139页
定价 49.90 元

投稿电话　(010)64027932　投稿信箱　tougao@cnmip.com.cn
营销中心电话　(010)64044283
冶金工业出版社天猫旗舰店　yjgycbs.tmall.com
（本书如有印装质量问题，本社营销中心负责退换）

Preface

By the time you open this book, you may be on your way to becoming a pilot. You should have the political character of loyalty and responsibility, the professional spirit of rigorous science, the work style of unity and cooperation, and the professional ethics of dedication, which is the sublimation of the fine tradition and spiritual culture formed in the long-term development practice of China civil aviation, which is considered as the spirit of contemporary civil aviation.

On the way to becoming a pilot, we should carry forward and practice the spirit of modern civil aviation, and strive to become flight professionals with a high sense of safety, rigorous scientific spirit and noble professional ethics, so as to provide support for the scientific and safe development of the industry.

In the post-epidemic era, the international aviation landscape has undergone significant changes, which requires pilots to master solid professional knowledge, have strong physical quality and good psychological quality, as well as international competitiveness, use English thinking and improve cross-cultural communication skills. The ability to construct a high-level thinking system for aviation safety decision making, identify unsafe factors and accurately assess the working status of flight crew; The comprehensive ability to optimize resource management, make flight decisions, and solve complex problems in flight are reflected in *Crew Resource Management course*.

The editor's basic idea in writing this book is to achieve the following three objectives:

(1) Knowledge objectives. Clearly understand the development history of flight crew resource management and international civil aviation norms, perceive the

cutting-edge trends and hot issues of civil aviation development, fully master the core theories, basic concepts and methods, and deeply understand the realization approach of efficient flight crew cooperation.

(2) Ability objectives. Use English thinking to improve cross-cultural communication ability; Construct the advanced thinking system of aviation safety decision, analyze and deduce civil aviation accident cases; Master ability to identify unsafe factors and accurately assess flight crew working conditions; Master comprehensive ability to optimize crew resource management, make flight decisions, and solve complex problems in flight.

(3) Value objectives. Pay attention to engineering ethics education and foster the spirit of civil aviation artisans to keep improving; Cultivate the feelings of home and country and the ambition of "serving the country by aviation", and stimulate the students'sense of belonging, mission and identity of civil aviation career.

The air transport industry needs flight personnel with advanced thinking of safe flight decision-making and comprehensive ability to deal with practical flight problems. The sequence of teaching modules of this book starts from problem solving and accident investigation to explore the components of flight resource unit management, analyze the reasons for the difference in management level, seek solutions, and finally form a flight decision model to complete evaluation and optimization. The main content is divided into six units: introduction to crew resource management, crew communication, situational awareness, pilot judgment and aeronautical decision making, cockpit leadership, cockpit automation. The logic fully considers the depth and breadth of the teaching content, integrates the basic principles and common methods of crew resource management, and completes the overall reconstruction of the curriculum content system. This kind of teaching logic helps to cultivate students'exploration and effectively adjusts students'participation enthusiasm.

In recent years, China's civil aviation is developing rapidly, and the dream of becoming a civil aviation power is being realized gradually through the unremitting efforts of generations of civil aviation staff, which has higher requirements on the international vision and English language ability of pilots. This book is written in both Chinese and English, which is an attempt in the field of crew resource management training. It's my great honor to take this opportunity to express my special thanks to Zhu Cong, Zhu Junlin, Gu Wen and Wang Siqi for their valuable comments during the preparation of this book.

Due to limitation of knowledge and experience, there will be deficiencies and omissions, please contact me if there is an error in the book.

The editor

February, 2022

前　言

当你翻开这本书的时候，你可能正在为成为一名飞行员思索着。你需具有忠诚担当的政治品格、严谨科学的专业精神、团结协作的工作作风、敬业奉献的职业操守，这是中国民航在长期发展实践中形成的优良传统和精神文化的升华，是当代民航精神。

在成为飞行员的路上，我们要弘扬和践行当代民航精神，努力成为具有高度安全意识，严谨科学精神和高尚职业道德的飞行专业人才，为行业科学发展、安全发展提供支撑。

后疫情时代的国际航空格局发生重要变化，这就要求飞行员除了掌握扎实的专业知识，具备强健的体能素质和良好的心理素质之外，还应具有国际竞争力，运用英语思维，提高跨文化交流的能力；构建航空安全决策的高级思维体系，识别不安全因素，准确评估飞行机组工作状态的能力；优化资源管理，制定飞行决策，解决飞行中复杂问题的综合能力，这些能力指标都在机组资源管理课程中有所体现。

编者编写本书的基本思路是实现以下三个目标：

（1）知识目标。明晰机组资源管理的发展历程和国际民航规范，察觉民航发展前沿动态和热点问题，全面掌握核心理论及基本概念、基本方法，深刻领会飞行机组高效合作的实现途径。

（2）能力目标。运用英语思维，提高跨文化交流能力；构建航空安全决策的高级思维体系，解析和推演民航事故案例；识别不安全因素，准确评估飞行机组工作状态的能力；优化资源管理，制定飞行决策，提高解决飞行中复杂问题的综合能力。

（3）价值目标。注重工程伦理教育，培育精益求精的民航工匠精神；树立家国情怀和“航空报国”志向，激发学生的民航职业归属感、使命感和认同感。

航空运输业需要具有安全飞行决策的高级思维和处置飞行实际问题的综合能力的飞行人员。本书的教学模块的先后顺序为从解决问题出发，从事故调查研究入手，探究机组资源股管理的组成要素，分析管理水平有差异的原因，寻求解决途径，最终形成飞行决策模型，完成评估和优化。主要内容分为6篇：机组资源管理概论、机组沟通与交流、情景意识、判断与决策、驾驶舱领导、驾驶舱自动化。这种逻辑充分考虑到教学内容的深度和广度，将机组资源股管理的基本原理和常用方法融入，完成课程内容体系的整体重构。这种授课逻辑有助于培养学生的探索性，有效调动学生的参与积极性。

近年来，中国民航正在快速发展，民航强国的梦想正在一代代民航人的不懈努力中逐步实现。结合对飞行人员的国际视野、英语语言能力都有更高的要求，本书采用中英文对照的形式编写，这是机组资源管理教学领域中的一次尝试。感谢朱聪、朱俊霖、顾问和王思奇在本书编写过程中提出的宝贵意见。

由于编者的学识水平有限，书中难免存在不妥和疏漏之处，希望同行专家和广大读者批评指正。

编　者

2022年2月

Contents

目　录

Unit 1

Introduction to Crew Resource Management

第 1 篇　机组资源管理概论

Lead-in
课程导入

"So if I hadn't used CRM①. , if we had not let everybody put their input in, it's a cinch we wouldn't have made it."

Alfred Haynes

Captain of United Airlines Flight 232 in1989

"如果我没有使用机组资源管理，如果我们没有让每个飞行员都参与进来，我们就不可能做到。"

阿尔弗雷德·海恩斯

1989 年美联航 232 航班机长

United Airlines Flight 232, flight scheduled to fly from Stapleton International Airport in Denver to O'Hare International Airport in Chicago on July 19, 1989, that crash-landed at Sioux Gateway Airport in Sioux City, Iowa, after the failure of its tail engine caused the loss of all hydraulic control of the plane; more than half of those aboard survived.

1989 年 7 月 19 日，美国联合航空公司 232 号航班按照飞行计划，从丹佛国际机场飞到芝加哥奥黑尔国际机场。由于位于尾翼的发动机损坏造成控制飞机的所有液压系统失效，在美国艾奥瓦州的苏城迫降，机上超过一半人员幸存。

The United Airlines McDonnell Douglas DC-10, carrying 285 passengers and 11 crew members, took off from Denver at 2: 09 pm. For the first hour, the flight was uneventful. However, at 3: 16 pm, a cracked fan blade in the rear engine disintegrated, causing the engine to fail, while flying debris severed all three hydraulic lines and pierced the horizontal stabilizer. People on the aircraft heard a loud bang, and the plane shuddered violently and began ascending and rolling to the right. The pilots, Captain Alfred Haynes and First Officer William Records, quickly discovered that neither the autopilot nor the manual controls had any effect. In desperation, Haynes closed the throttle to the left engine and pushed all the power to the right, and the aircraft righted itself.

这架载有 285 名乘客和 11 名机组人员的联合航空公司 DC-10 飞机于下午 2 点 09 分从丹佛起飞。飞行最开始的一个小时里平安无事。然而，下午 3 点 16 分，位于尾翼处的发动机的一个风扇叶片破裂，导致发动机故障，碎片损坏了机上所有三套液压系统（碎片切断了三套液压系统的管路），刺穿了飞机的水平安定面。飞机上的人听到一声巨响，飞机剧烈地抖动，开始上升并向右翻滚。机长海恩斯机长和副驾驶很快发现，飞机的自动驾驶和手动控制都不起任何作用。在绝望中，海恩斯关闭了左侧引擎，收回了左侧引擎的推力，把所有的动力都推到右侧，飞机自己恢复了平衡。

The crew notified Minneapolis Air Traffic Control of the emergency, and it was determined that the plane should attempt to land at the airport at Sioux City. Dennis Fitch, a United Airlines

① CRM is originally short for cockpit resource management, now is for crew resource management.
CRM 这一术语早期是驾驶舱资源管理的缩写，后改为机组资源管理。

DC-10 training instructor, was a passenger in the first-class section, and he volunteered to help. Haynes instructed Fitch to operate the thrusters that powered the two remaining engines, which gave very minimal control over the aircraft's direction and orientation, while he and Records sought to get the normal flight controls working. Fitch found that the aircraft had a pronounced tendency to turn to the right.

机组人员通知了明尼阿波利斯空中交通管制中心这一紧急情况，并决定试图让飞机在苏城机场降落。美国联合航空 DC-10 教员丹尼斯·费奇当时坐在头等舱中，他挺身而出为机组助力。海恩斯机长指令费奇负责操作剩余两台发动机的推力，极其有限地调整飞行方向，而他和副驾驶则试图控制飞机。费奇发现这架飞机有明显的右转倾向。

Flight 232 proceeded in a series of barely controlled right spirals toward Sioux City. At 3：46 Fitch succeeded in using the thrusters to pull the plane enough to the left to approach the airport, and the crew then managed to get the plane lined up with a closed runway. The aircraft descended far too steeply and much too fast, and it tilted as it landed. The right wing struck the ground first and broke off. The tail section and the cockpit also broke off as the plane bounced several times.

232 航班几乎无法控制地向右盘旋，朝着苏城飞去。3 点 46 分，费奇成功地使用推力将飞机向左拉了足够的裕度，进行进近。随即，机组人员设法让飞机在一条封闭的跑道上对准跑道准备完成着陆。飞机下降速度过大，降落时呈倾斜状态。飞机右翼首先撞地并折断，飞机的尾翼和驾驶舱也在飞机几次弹起的过程中断裂。

In every aircraft accident there is a chain of events, known as the "accident chain" . Like falling dominoes, the chain starts with one event, decision or action, which leads to the next ultimately leading to the occurrence.

每一次飞机事故都是由一系列的事件造成的，这些事件被称为“事故链”。就像倒下的多米诺骨牌一样，这个链条从一个事件、决定或行动开始，然后引发下一个，最终导致这个事件的发生。

In the case of United 232 that chain started in the early 1970's during the manufacturing process of the engine fan disk, through the subsequent maintenance inspections, and finally the component failure which lead to the uncontained explosion. However, a separate chain of events and circumstances, some of which were quite fortuitous, lead to the high survival rate. This chain starts with the flight crew's use of Crew Resource Management, or CRM. Haynes credits the use of CRM as being one of the main factors that enabled the crew to guide the stricken DC-10 back to an airport. In a speech given at NASA's Ames Research Center in 1991, Haynes said "Up until 1980, we kind of worked on the concept that the captain was the authority on the aircraft. What he said, goes. And we lost a few airplanes because of that. Sometimes the captain isn't as smart as we thought he was. So why would I know more about getting that airplane on the ground under those conditions than the other three. So if I hadn't used [CRM], if we had not let everybody put their input in, it's a cinch we wouldn't have made it."

在联合航空 232 航班的案例中，这条事故链条开始于 20 世纪 70 年代初的发动机风扇生产制造的过程，继而是飞机维修检查环节，最终是由部件失效导致的无法控制的事故。然而，在一系列独立的事件和环境中，也存在一些非常偶然的事件，这些偶然挽救了这起事故中的大多数人的生命，我们要从机组人员使用机组资源管理（CRM）开始说起。海恩斯认为 CRM 的使用是使机组人员能够将出现故障的 DC-10 返回地面的主要原因之一。1991 年，海恩斯在美国宇航局艾姆斯研究中心的一次演讲中说：“直到 1980 年，我们都认为机长是飞行的权威。他说什么，飞行员就做什么。因此，我们损失了几架飞机。有时机长并不像人们想象中的那么聪明。为什么我比其他三个人更了解如何在这种特殊情况下让飞机着陆呢？如果我没有使用机组资源管理（CRM），如果我们没有让每个飞行员都参与进来，我们是不可能做到的。”

Key words

关键词

DC-10	美国道格拉斯公司研制的三发动机中远程宽机身客机，现已停产
fan blade	风扇叶片
closed runway	关闭的跑道
accident chain	事故链
Crew Resource Management（CRM）	机组资源管理

Discussion

讨论

（1） What is the function of hydraulic system? What will happen if all the onboard hydraulic systems fail?

（1） 液压系统的作用是什么？如果液压系统全部失效会引发什么后果？

（2） What shall you do if you were the captain of United 232?

（2） 如果你是美国联合航空 232 航班的机长，你会如何处置？

（3） What is Crew Resource Management? Why do you think it played such an important role of the high survival rate in that accident?

（3） 什么是机组资源管理？为什么机组资源管理能在此事故中挽救多人生命？

Advanced thinking
高阶思维

Function:
功能：
Components:
组成：
Evaluation:
评价：

Draw the chain of this accident.
画出本次事故的事故链。

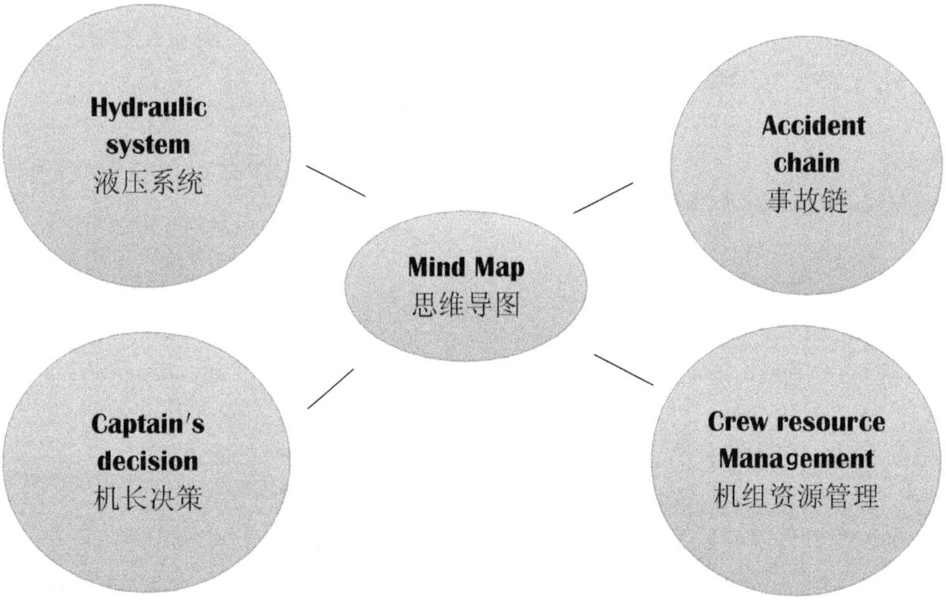

Step 1:
Step 2:
Step 3:
⋮
第一步：
第二步：
第三步：
⋮

How do you consider about Captain Haynes' operation?
你认为海恩斯机长的处置如何？

Components:
组成部分：

Function:
作用：

Lesson 1 Basic Concept of Crew Resource Management
第 1 课 机组资源管理基本概念

1.1 Definition
1.1 定义

John K. Lauber (1984), a psychologist member of the National Transportation Safety Board (NTSB), has defined CRM as "using all available resources information, equipment, and people to achieve safe and efficient flight operations". CRM includes optimizing not only the person-machine interface and the acquisition of timely, appropriate information, but also interpersonal activities including leadership, effective team formation and maintenance, problem-solving, decision-making, and maintaining situational awareness. Thus training in CRM involves communicating basic knowledge of human factors concepts that relate to aviation and providing the tools necessary to apply these concepts operationally. It represents a new focus on crew-level (as opposed to individual-level) aspects of training and operations.

1984 年，美国国家运输安全委员会（NTSB）的心理学家 John K. Lauber 将 CRM 定义为"使用所有可用的资源、信息、设备和人员来实现安全高效的飞行操作"。CRM 不仅包括人机界面的优化，获取及时、适当的信息，还包括人际交往中诸多因素，如领导力、团队组建和团队精神的体现、解决飞行问题、决策制定和保持情景意识。因此，CRM 的培训包括学习掌握航空领域内有关人的因素的基本知识，以及提供必要的工具完成基于基本知识的实际飞行操作，培训更加关注整体、团队而不是个人表现。

1.2 Generations
1.2 发展阶段

1.2.1 First Generation: Cockpit Resource Management
1.2.1 第一代：驾驶舱资源管理

The first comprehensive U. S. CRM program was initiated by United Airlines in 1981. The training was developed with the aid of consultants who had developed training programs for corporations trying to enhance managerial effectiveness. The United program was modeled closely on a form of training called the "Managerial Grid" developed by psychologists Robert Blake and Jane Mouton (Blake & Mouton, 1964).

在美国，美国联合航空公司在 1981 年率先发起了 CRM 培训。这些 CRM 培训是在有多年为企业提供咨询服务的顾问团的帮助下进行的，培训的目的是提高管理效率。美国联合航空公司的项目模仿了心理学家罗伯特·布莱克和简·莫顿在 1964 年提出的一种名为“管理网格”的培训形式。

The Blake Mouton "Managerial Grid" is based on basically two behavioral dimensions:

First being the concern for people; it is a measure wherein a leader takes into account his or her team members'demands, needs, interests and also their areas of personal development. It is usually done when the leader has to decide ways to accomplish tasks and desired goals for the organization.

Second is the concern for results; it is an extent to which a leader focusses on concrete tasks and objectives, ensuring greater efficiency for the organization and high productivity. It is also done at the time when the leader has to decide how to accomplish the results from a task best.

布莱克·莫顿“管理网格”主要基于两个行为维度：

首先是对人的关心：团队领导者将团队成员的需求、需要、兴趣和他们的个人发展领域纳入考量。通常用于领导者必须决定如何完成任务和实现组织预期目标的时候。

其次是对业绩的关心：团队领导者专注于具体任务和目标的达成程度，以确保效率和业绩，通常被用于当领导者必须决定完成一项任务的最佳途径的时候。

The training was conducted in an intensive seminar setting and included participants' diagnoses of their own managerial style. Other airline programs in this era also drew heavily on management training approaches. These programs emphasized changing individual styles and correcting deficiencies in individual behavior such as a lack of assertiveness by juniors and authoritarian behavior by captains.

培训的方式是密集的研讨会，研讨内容包括参与者对自己管理风格的诊断。在那个历史时代中，航空公司其他培训项目也大量采用了管理方法培训作为核心。这些项目强调改变个人风格，纠正个人行为中的不足，如下级缺乏直陈性和机长的高权威性的表现。

Supporting this emphasis, the National Transportation Safety Board had singled out the captain's failure to accept input from junior crewmembers and a lack of The Evolution of Crew Resource Management assertiveness by the flight engineer as causal factors in a United Airlines crash in 1978. First generation courses were psychological in nature, with a heavy focus on psychological testing and general concepts such as leadership.

美国国家运输安全委员会（National Transportation Safety Board）指出，1978 年美国联合航空公司（United Airlines）坠机事件的原因就是机长未能接受低阶段机组成员的意见，以及飞行工程师缺乏直陈性。第一代 CRM，本质上侧重心理因素，强调心理测试和基础概念，包括领导力等。

They advocated general strategies of interpersonal behavior without providing clear definitions of appropriate behavior in the cockpit.

他们提倡了普遍的人际交往行为策略，却没有给出针对驾驶舱中的恰当行为的明确定义。

In addition to classroom training, some programs also included full mission simulator training

(Line Oriented Flight Training) where crews could practice interpersonal skills without jeopardy.

除了课堂训练以外，一些 CRM 培训项目还包括全任务模拟器训练，即面向航线的飞行训练，机组人员可以在没有飞行危险的前提下练习驾驶舱的沟通交流技能。

Here is a LOFT example.

此处有一个面向航线的飞行训练范例。

Boarding (Flight crew flight preparation: route CDU input, simulated communication)

登机（飞行机组飞行直接准备：航路 CDU 输入，模拟沟通）

Pre-flight checklist

飞行前检查单

Departure airport and destination airport weather condition、alternate airport choice、route、accumulated ice、turbulence、thunderstorm、circling

起飞机场和目的地机场天气情况、备降机场选择、航路、积冰、颠簸、雷雨、绕飞

Push back

推出

Check list before startup

启动前检查单

Engine start

启动发动机

Checklist before taxi

滑行前检查单

Tower: Instruction, taxiway, runway, take off

塔台：给出指令，可以滑出，进跑道，起飞

Checklist before take off

起飞前检查单

Simulator, take off, takeoff configuration

模拟机，起飞，设置起飞构型

Checklist after takeoff

起飞后检查单

Climb

爬升

Cruise

巡航

Emergency Situation: depressurization

特情：失压

The instructions given by instructor /blasting sounds

教员给出指令/爆破声响

Identify depressurization

识别出失压

Perform non-standard checklists for emergency situations
针对特情执行非正常检查单
Communication with cabin and dispatch
与客舱沟通及公司签派人员沟通
Canin
与客舱
(1) Depressurization. (2) Anyone hurt or any aircraft damage. (3) Plan (ferry, Alternae).
(1) 飞机失压。(2) 询问有无人或飞机损伤。(3) 告知客舱下一步飞行计划 (返场, 备降)。
Dispatch
与签派
(1) Flight status. (2) Next decision: ground assistance (suggestions, such as Hefei or Nanjing if it is not convenient for alternate landing in Hangzhou).
(1) 航班状况。(2) 下一步决策: 地面给予援助 (签派给出建议, 比如杭州不方便备降, 可以去合肥或南京)。
ATC
与管制
Whole LOFT process, emergency descent to 3000 feet (plain)
整个 LOFT 过程, 紧急下降高度 3000 英尺 (平原)
Prepare approach check list before landing
着陆前准备
Approach checklist
进近检查单
Descent checklist
下降检查单
Complete final ILS approach
五边完成盲降进近
Complete landing checklist
完成着陆检查单
Checklist before landing
落地检查单
Landing
降落

1.2.2 Second Generation: Crew Resource Management
1.2.2 第二代: 机组资源管理

NASA held another workshop for the industry in 1986. By this time a growing number of airlines in the U. S. and around the world had initiated CRM training and many reported on their programs. One of the conclusions drawn by working groups at the meeting was that explicit (or stand alone) CRM training would ultimately disappear as a separate component of training when it became imbedded in the fabric of flight training and flight operations.

1986 年，NASA 为航空业的发展举办了一次研讨会。彼时，包括美国在内的世界范围内越来越多的航空公司都开始了 CRM 培训，许多公司在会上都汇报了他们的项目。工作组在会议上得出的一个结论是，CRM 应该和飞行训练以及飞行操作有机结合，不能孤立进行。

At the same time, a new generation of CRM courses was beginning to emerge. Accompanying a change in the emphasis of training to focus on cockpit group dynamics was a change in name from Cockpit to Crew Resource Management. The new courses, typified by the program developed by Delta Airlines dealt with more specific aviation concepts related to flight operations and became more modular as well as more team oriented in nature.

与此同时，新一代的 CRM 课程开始出现。随着培训重点的转变，其名称也从驾驶舱改为机组资源管理。以达美航空公司开发的培训项目为代表的新课程，着眼于飞行操作相关的更具体的航空概念的阐述，其训练在本质上变得更加模块化，且更注重团队。

Basic training conducted in intensive seminars included concepts such as team building, briefing strategies, situational awareness and stress management. Specific modules addressed decision making strategies.

基本训练包括团队建设、简令策略、情景意识和压力管理等概念，具体的模块涉及飞行决策。

1.2.3　Third Generation: CRM-broadening the Scope

1.2.3　第三代：公司资源管理

In the early 1990s, CRM training began to proceed down multiple paths. Training began to reflect characteristics of the aviation system in which crews must function, including the multiple input factors such as organizational culture that determine safety.

在 20 世纪 90 年代早期，CRM 培训开始向复合型发展。训练内容涉及飞行系统的各项特征，包括决定飞行安全的航空公司组织文化等多种因素。

At the same time, efforts began to integrate CRM with technical training and to focus on specific skills and behaviors that pilots could use to function more effectively. Several airlines began to include modules addressing CRM issues in the use of flightdeck automation. Programs also began to address the recognition and assessment of human factors issues.

与此同时，CRM 培训开始努力与技术培训相结合，并将重点放在飞行员可以更有效地使用某种特定技能和操作上。几家航空公司开始在使用驾驶舱自动化时加入 CRM 训练模块。培训项目也开始实现对人为因素的识别和评估。

Accompanying this was the initiation of advanced training in CRM for check airmen and others responsible for training, reinforcement, and evaluation of technical and human factors. Accompanying this greater specificity in training for flight crews, CRM began to be extended to other groups within airlines such as flight attendants, dispatchers, and maintenance personnel.

Many airlines began to conduct joint cockpit-cabin CRM training.

与此同时，开始对检查员和其他负责技术及人为因素的培训、强化和评估的专业人员进行 CRM 培训。随着对机组人员的培训更加具体化，CRM 开始扩展到航空公司的其他群体，如空乘人员、签派人员和维修人员。许多航空公司开始开展驾驶舱与客舱联合 CRM 培训。

A number of carriers also developed specialized CRM training for new captains to focus on the leadership role that accompanies command. While third generation courses filled a recognized need to extend the concept of the flight crew, they may also have had the unintended consequence of diluting the original focus on the reduction of human error.

一部分航空承运人针对新机长开发出了专门的 CRM 培训，专注于与机组资源管理相关的领导力培训。第三代 CRM 扩展了机组的概念，同时减少了对人为错误的关注。

1.2.4　Fourth Generation: CRM-integration and Proceduralization

1.2.4　第四代：整合化和程序化的机组资源管理

The Federal Aviation Administration introduced a major change in the training and qualification of flight crews in 1990 with the initiation of its Advanced Qualification Program. AQP is a voluntary program that allows air carriers to develop innovative training that fits the needs of the specific organization. In exchange for this greater flexibility in training, carriers are required to provide both CRM and LOFT for all flight crews and to integrate CRM concepts into technical training. Most of the major U. S. airlines and several regional carriers are transitioning into AQP from the older model expressed in Federal Aviation Regulations, Parts 121 and 135.

联邦航空管理局在 1990 年对飞行人员的培训和认定进行了重大改革，启动了高级资格大纲（AQP）。AQP 具有很强的自主性，允许航空公司航空承运人开发符合特定组织需要的创新训练。为了获得更大的培训适应性，航空公司需要为所有机组人员提供 CRM 培训和面向航向的飞行训练，并将 CRM 概念融入技术培训中。美国大多数主要航空公司和几家地区性航空公司正在从联邦航空法规第 121 部和 135 部中原有的训练模式过渡到 AQP。

To complete the shift to AQP, carriers are required to complete detailed analyses of training requirements for each aircraft and to develop programs that address the human factors (CRM) issues in each aspect of training. As part of the integration of CRM, several airlines have begun to proceduralize the concepts involved by adding specific behaviors to their checklists.

为了完成向 AQP 的转变，航空公司需要完成对每架飞机的培训需求的详细分析，并开发解决培训各个方面的人为因素（CRM）问题的项目。作为 CRM 整合化的一部分，一些航空公司已经开始将涉及的概念程序化，将具体的行为添加到检查单中。

The goal is to ensure that decisions and actions are informed by consideration of "bottom lines" and that the basics of CRM are observed, particularly in non-standard situations. On the surface, the fourth generation of CRM would seem to solve the problems of human error by making CRM an integral part of all flight training. Although empirical data are not yet available, there is general consensus among U. S. airlines that the AQP approach yields improvements in the training and qualification of flight crews.

这样做的目标是确保飞行员的决策和行动都是基于“底线”的充分考虑之上，特别是注意到非标准情形中的 CRM 基础知识。从表面上看，第四代 CRM 似乎解决了人为错误的问题，使 CRM 成为所有飞行训练的一个组成部分。虽然还没有充足的试验依据，但美国航空公司普遍认为，AQP 方法可以提高机组人员的训练质量和飞行机组的素质。

1.2.5　Fifth Generation：CRM-error Management

1.2.5　第五代：差错管理

The primary idea of this generation is the Human Error, which is strongly believed that the thing makes CRM so distinct is the Error Management. It is well known that Human Errors are in the man's nature however, errors may turn to a valuable source of collecting information. After collecting and analyzing this information, an effective way of reducing the errors, must be chosen. The most effective manner found was the so called error management troika.

这一代 CRM 训练的主要内容是研究人为错误，人们坚信，差错管理是使 CRM 与其他领域明显区别的主要原因。众所周知，人犯错误是人的本性，错误可成为收集信息的一个有价值的来源。在收集和分析这些信息之后，人们必须选择一种有效地减少差错的方法，其中最有效的方法是使用避免错误的三道防线。

According to troika, there are three steps of defense：avoid error, trap error before occurring and mitigate the consequences when an error has occurred or not trapped.

这三道防线分别是避免错误、在错误发生前阻止、减轻已发生的错误带来的后果。

1.2.6　Sixth Generation：CRM- threat and Error Management (TEM)

1.2.6　第六代：威胁及差错管理

Threat and error management (TEM) is a systems approach to aviation safety originally developed by human factors researchers at the University of Texas. TEM competencies are now embraced by airlines worldwide and recognized as an international best practice by, among others, the International Civil Aviation Organization, the European Aviation Safety Authority, the International Air Transport Association, the National Air Transport Association, and the U. S. Federal Aviation Administration. TEM offers an intuitive and flexible approach to practical risk management.

威胁和差错管理（TEM）是一种航空安全系统方法，最初是由得克萨斯大学的人为因素研究人员开发的。TEM 能力现在被世界各地的航空公司所接受，并被国际民用航空组织、欧洲航空安全局、国际航空运输协会、国家航空运输协会和美国联邦航空管理局等认可。威胁和差错管理（TEM）为风险管理提供了一种非常实用且直观灵活的方法。

Threats are defined as "events or errors that occur beyond the influence of the flight crew, increase operational complexity, and which must be managed to maintain the margins of safety". They increase the operational complexity of a flight. Require crew attention and management if safety margins are to be maintained.

威胁是指在飞行期间应加以注意和应对的外部事件或差错。它们增加了飞行的操作复杂性，飞行员应加以注意和管理才能保持飞行的安全裕度。

(1) External threats.

Those outside of our direct control.

(e. g. , weather, lack of equipment, hard to understand documentation, results of others' errors, inadequate lighting)

(1) 外部威胁。

那些不受控制的因素。

(例如，天气、设备不足、文件难以理解、他人错误导致的结果、照明不足)

(2) Internal threats.

Those within our control.

(e. g. , fatigue, proficiency, situation awareness, stress)

(2) 内部威胁。

那些在我们控制范围内的。

(例如，疲劳、熟练、情境意识、压力)

Error is a crew action or inaction that leads to a deviation from crew or organizational intentions or expectations.

差错指偏离机组意图或预期的机组成员的行为或既定工作的错、漏、忘的现象。

There are 5 types of errors:

(1) Intentional non-compliance errors.

(2) Procedural errors.

(3) Communication errors.

(4) Proficiency errors.

(5) Operational decision errors.

差错可以分为五种，分别是：

(1) 违规错误。

(2) 程序错误。

(3) 交流沟通错误。

(4) 熟练性错误。

(5) 飞行决策错误。

Threat and error management (TEM) offers an intuitive and flexible approach to practical risk management. The Threat and Error Management (TEM) model is a conceptual framework that assists in understanding, from an operational perspective, the inter-relationship between safety and human performance in dynamic and challenging operational contexts, as shown in Figure 1-1.

威胁与错误管理（TEM）提供了一种进行风险管理的直观灵活的实用方法。TEM 模型是一个帮助人们理解的概念框架，从操作的角度帮助理解安全之间的相互关系以及在动态和具有挑战性的操作环境中的人的表现，如图 1-1 所示。

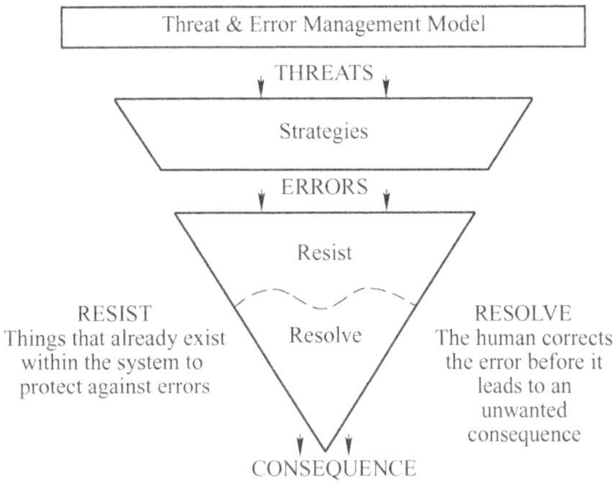

Figure 1-1　Threat & error management model

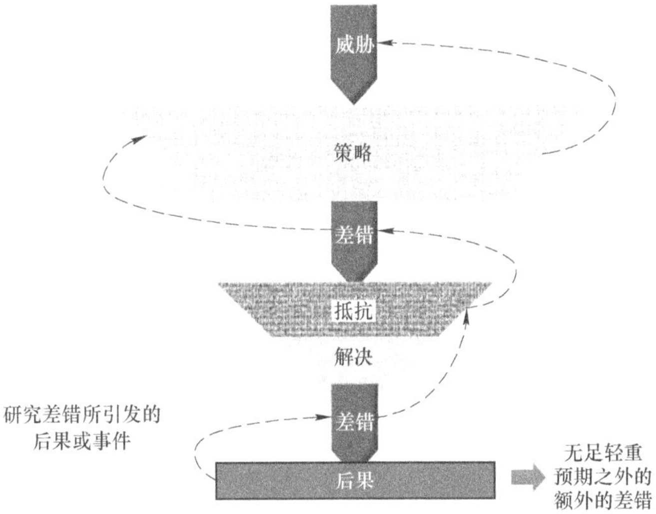

图 1-1　威胁与差错管理模型

扫一扫查看彩图

Lesson 2 Basic Components and Models
第2课 组成部分和理论模型

2.1 The SHEL Model
2.1 SHEL 模型

The concept (the name being derived from the initial letters of its components: Software, Hardware, Environment, Liveware) was first developed by Edwards in 1972, with a modified diagram to illustrate the model developed by Hawkins in 1975. The model is often depicted in diagrammatic form as shown in Figure 2-1.

SHEL 模型 1972 年由英国学者爱德华提出，并于 1975 年由霍金斯图表化——以其组件名称的首字母命名：软件、硬件、环境和人。模型通常以图 2-1 所示的图表形式进行描述。

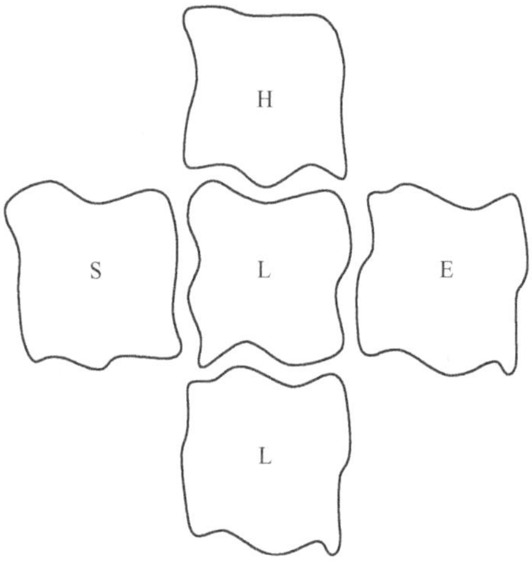

Figure 2-1 SHEL model

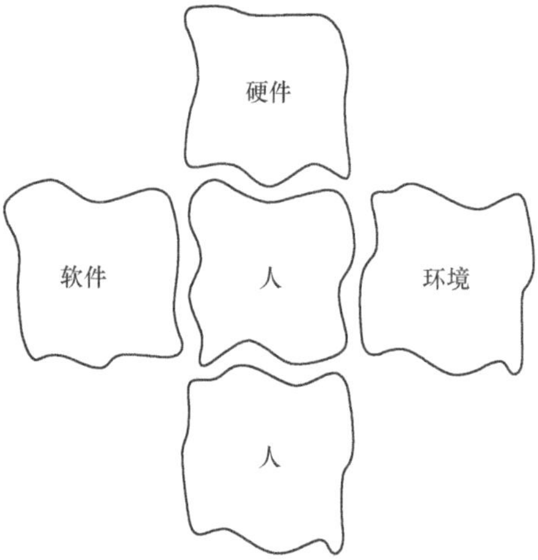

图 2-1 SHEL 模型

One practical diagram to illustrate this conceptual model uses blocks to represent the different components of Human Factors.

- **Software**—the rules, procedures, written documents etc., which are part of the standard operating procedures.
- **Hardware**—It is comprised of the actual cockpit, the layout of flight controls, seat design and computer systems.
- **Environment**—The social and economic climate as well as the natural environment.
- **Liveware**— Controllers, flight crews, engineers and maintenance personnel,

management and administration people-within in the system.

这个概念模型使用了一个用图块构成实用图表表示“人为因素”的不同组成部分。

- **软件**——规则、程序、书面文件等，它们是标准操作程序的一部分。
- **硬件**——驾驶舱、飞行控制、座椅设计和计算机系统组成。
- **环境**——社会、经济环境以及自然环境等。
- **人**——航空系统内的管制员、机组人员、工程师和机务人员、管理和行政人员。

According to the SHEL model, a mismatch between the Liveware and other four components contributes to human error. Thus, these interactions must be assessed and considered in all sectors of the aviation system.

根据 SHEL 模型，人和其他四个组件之间的不匹配导致了人为错误。因此，必须在航空系统的所有部门内针对该模型进行评估和考虑这些部分之间的相互作用。

Liveware

The critical focus of the model is the human participant, or liveware, the most critical as well as the most flexible component in the system. The edges of this block are not simple and straight, and so the other components of the system must be carefully matched to them if stress in the system and eventual breakdown are to be avoided.

人

模型的关键焦点是人，这是系统中最关键也是最灵活的组件。这个块体的边缘不是平直的，因此，如果要避免系统中的故障，系统的其他部分必须小心地与人进行匹配。

However, of all the dimensions in the model, this is the one which is least predictable and most susceptible to the effects of internal (hunger, fatigue, motivation, etc.) and external (temperature, light, noise, workload, etc.) changes.

然而，在模型中的所有维度中，人最不可预测，最容易受到内部（饥饿、疲劳、动机等）和外部（温度、光线、噪声、工作量等）变化的影响。

Liveware—Liveware

This is the interface between people. In this interface, we are concerned with leadership, co-operation, teamwork and personality interactions. It includes programmes like Crew Resource Management (CRM), Line Oriented Flight Training (LOFT) etc.

人—人

这是人与人之间的界面。在这个界面中，我们关注的是领导力、合作、团队合作和个性互动。它包括机组资源管理（CRM）、面向航线的飞行训练（LOFT）等项目。

Liveware—Software

Software is the collective term which refers to all the laws, rules, regulations, orders, standard operating procedures, customs and conventions and the normal way in which things are done. Increasingly, software also refers to the computer-based programmes developed to operate the automated systems.

人—软件

软件是所有法律、规则、规章、命令、标准操作程序、习惯和惯例以及做事的正常方式的统称。逐渐地，软件也指为操作自动化系统而开发的以计算机为基础的程序。

In order to achieve a safe, effective operation between the liveware and software it is important to ensure that the software, particularly if it concerns rules and procedures, is capable of being implemented.

为了在人和软件之间实现安全、有效的操作，重要的是要确保软件，特别是涉及规则和程序的软件能够被执行。

Liveware—Hardware

Another interactive component of the SHEL model is the interface between liveware and hardware. This interface is the one most commonly considered when speaking of human-machine systems: design of seats to fit the sitting characteristics of the human body, of displays to match the sensory and information processing characteristics of the user, of controls with proper movement, coding and location.

As an example the press to talk switch is a hardware component which interfaces with liveware. The switch will have been designed to meet a number of expectations, including the probability that when it is pressed the controller has a live line to talk. Similarly, switches should have been positioned in locations that can be easily accessed by controllers in various situations and the manipulation of equipment should not impede the reading of displayed information or other devices which might need to be used at the same time.

人—硬件

SHEL 模型的另一个交互组件是人和硬件之间。当谈到人机系统时，座椅的设计要符合人体的坐姿特征，显示器要符合用户的感官和信息处理特征，控制装置要有适当的运动模式、编码方式和位置。

以按下发话电门为例，它是一种与实时人与硬件之间的互动。该电门的设计将满足多种预期，包括按下电门时即可通话。同样，电门应该被放置在控制者可以轻松访问的位置，设备的操作不应妨碍读取显示的信息或其他可能需要同时使用的设备。

Liveware —Environment

The liveware-environment interface refers to those interactions which may be out of the direct control of humans, namely the physical environment-temperature, weather, etc. , but within which aircraft operate. The appropriate matching of the liveware-environmental interactions involve a wide array of disparate disciplines, from environmental studies, physiology, psychology through to physics and engineering.

人—环境

这个界面是指那些可能不受人的直接控制，但影响飞机运行，即物理环境—温度、天气等。人—环境互动的适当匹配涉及许多不同学科，环境学、生理学、心理学到物理学和工程学都有涉及。

2.2 Case Study
2.2 案例分析

Try to use SHEL model to discuss with your mates about this accident.

试着用 SHEL 模型和你的同伴一起分析以下空难。

On February 6, 1996, Bergen Air Flight 301, a Boeing 757-23A operated by Bergen Air, a Turkish charter company, veered to the left and plunged into the sea five minutes after takeoff from Santo Domingo, the capital of the Dominican Republic. All 189 people on board, including the crew, no one survived.

伯根航空 301 号班机是隶属土耳其包机公司伯根航空，执飞机型是波音 757-23A，1996 年 2 月 6 日，飞机在多米尼加共和国首都圣多明哥起飞后五分钟突然向左倾侧，摔进海里，机上 189 人（含机组成员），无一生还。

On that day, the flight to Frankfurt broke down and the ground staff went to the ramp to find a replacement plane. Bergen Had a Boeing 757 that had been sitting on the ramp for more than three weeks when it was ordered to make the flight. At 11：03 pm, Flight 301 was cleared to leave the gate and taxi on the runway. Just then, the captain noticed that his airspeed gauge was too slow and asked the co-pilot to tell him the speed.

当日，原本飞往法兰克福的班机故障，地勤人员至机坪寻找替代飞机。正好伯根航空有一架波音 757 已在机坪内待了三个多星期，便受命进行此次飞行。晚上 11 时 03 分，301 号班机获准离开登机门，在跑道上滑行；就在此时，机长发现他的空速表过慢，于是要求副驾驶告知速度。

But after takeoff, the pilot's airspeed indicator sped up, the co-pilot's slowed down, and the flight crew was confused by conflicting emergency signals from the flight management computer such as rudder ratio, overspeed, too low speed and too low altitude. The captain pulled back the throttle to reduce the speed of the plane, which was indicated by an onboard alarm.

起飞以后，机长的空速表加速了，副机长的却慢了下来，飞行管理计算机也发出矛盾紧急信号，譬如方向舵比率、超速、速度太低及飞行高度太低等，把机组员弄得一头雾水。由于飞机上的警报指示飞机速度过高，于是机长收油门减速。

The plane was in stall, but they were not able to accurately observe the speed of the plane and its vertical speed. As a result, the plane's altitude is falling at a rapid rate, but there is no corresponding change in the altimeter. Although the altimeter indicated 2000 feet, the actual height was less than 500 feet. At that point, the plane's No. 1 engine stopped, causing the plane to tip to the left and roll over. The crew were unable to stop the descent and the plane crashed heavily into the sea about five minutes after takeoff. The investigation is being led by the Dominican Bureau of Investigation, assisted by the US National Transportation Safety Board (NTSB). Local searchers, aided by the U. S. Navy, were able to retrieve the plane's black boxes from 7200 feet of the ocean floor shortly after the crash. A subsequent crash investigation revealed that the main cause of the instrument error was damage to or blockage of the Pitot tube underneath the plane's exterior. The function of the pitot tube is to provide the airspeed of the aircraft in flight. If it is blocked, the airspeed indicator will provide error information to the crew.

此时飞机正在失速，但是他们不能够准确地观察判读飞机的飞行速度及垂直上升速度。结果飞机的飞行高度正急剧损失，但高度表却没有出现任何相应的改变。虽然当时高度计指着 2000 英尺，但实际高度却不到 500 英尺。此时，飞机的一号引擎停止运作，客机向左倾侧，继而翻滚。机组人员完全没法控制飞机停止下降，飞机大约在起飞的 5 分钟之后重重摔进海里。事故由多米尼加的调查局负责调查，美国国家运输安全委员会（NTSB）协助。当地搜寻人员获得美国海军协助，于空难发生后三星期于 7200 英尺深海底打捞出失事客机的黑匣子。其后的空难原因调查揭示仪器发生错误的主要原因是位于飞机驾驶舱外下方的皮托管（pitot tube）受损或被堵塞。皮托管的功用是提供飞机飞行时的空速，一旦被堵塞，空速表便会提供错误信息给机组。

It is not known why the pitot tube was blocked because the wreckage could not be retrieved. Investigators found that ground staff at the airport never put a protective cap on the passenger jet's pipette during the three-week stay at the airport. Although this would rule out the possibility that a passenger plane's pitot tube was sealed by a protective cap during take off, it would also violate aviation rules. Because the aircraft is idle at the airport or waiting for a mission, must add a protective cover for the pitot tube.

由于没法打捞残骸，因此皮托管为何被堵塞仍是未知数。调查人员发现，机场的地勤人员在出事客机停留在机场的三星期内，从来没有为该客机的皮托管套上保护套。虽然这样可以排除客机的皮托管在起飞时被保护套封住的可能性，但这种做法同样也违反航空安全守则。按规定，飞机在机场被闲置或等候任务时，必须为皮托管加上保护套。

A local wasp, Sceliphron caementarium (mud bees, as the locals call it), has a habit of building mud nests inside tubes and can be found everywhere, including airports. So investigators believe the insect most likely built its nest in the plane's unprotected pitot tube while the plane was parked on the tarmac.

在当地有一种名称为 Sceliphron caementarium 的胡蜂（当地人称为泥蜂），喜欢在管状物内用泥土筑巢，而且这种胡蜂在当地可以说无处不在，当然包括机场。因此调查员认为飞机停在停机坪时，这种昆虫在飞机没有受保护的皮托管内筑巢。

In addition, the crew is also responsible for the crash. The captain did not abort the takeoff when he discovered that his airspeed gauge was faulty. And after a series of mistakes, the final airliner into the point of no salvation. Why didn't the captain abort takeoff? Due to the night of the accident, the local weather was unstable and raining, so the captain may have feared that the plane was running at high speed, coupled with the wet runway, so the captain did not dare to risk stopping the plane. But the most likely reason is that the plane was in the area for more than three weeks with its crew, making them so homesick that they took off knowing the instrument problem was minor. About a minute after takeoff, the plane's elevation increased after the crew put the plane on autopilot, a condition that occurs when the aircraft's airspeed is too high and the autopilot system raises the nose to slow it down. However, the autopilot system only responded to the information displayed by the instrument on the plane. Although the pilot's airspeed indicator indicated that the plane was exceeding the speed limit, in fact, the decreasing speed of the co-pilot's airspeed indicator reflected the real condition of the plane at that time. The captain ignored the co-pilot's airspeed indicator and recklessly pulled the throttle back, causing the plane to stall.

另外，机组也应为这起空难负责。当机长发现他的空速表有故障时，并没有终止起飞。之后的一连串失误，终令客机进入无可挽救的地步。为什么机长当初没有放弃起飞？由于出事当晚，当地天气不稳且下着雨，机长认为飞机在湿滑的跑道上高速滑跑过程中不能冒险刹停飞机。但最可能的原因是，该飞机连同机组成员待在当地足足三星期多，令机组成员思乡心切，于是明知飞机仪表故障，却认为只是小问题而强行起飞。飞机起飞后约一分钟，机组将飞机设定为自动飞行状态后出现仰角过大的情况，出现这种状态是因为飞机空速过高，自动驾驶系统便会抬高机头以达到减速效果。但自动驾驶系统只是以机上的仪表显示的信息给予反应，虽然当时机长的空速表显示飞机超速，可是实际上，副驾驶的空速表所显示的速度不断减少，却反映了飞机当时的真正状况。机长却忽略了副驾驶的空速仪表，因而鲁莽地将油门往后收，结果导致飞机失速。

When the plane stalled, the co-pilot and the second pilot suggested to the captain that the plane should be nose-down and in a nose-down position to stop the descent by allowing air to flow under the wings to create lift, but the captain did not respond at all to these suggestions. Perhaps the captain was confused, or perhaps the captain thought he had considerable experience of flying a 757, and his pride made him ignore the advice of a junior co-pilot with only 75 hours of experience. In any case, they missed enough altitude to save the plane, killing 189 people.

当飞机失速时，副驾驶及另一位副驾驶曾向机长建议让飞机机头朝下，让飞机以俯冲姿态，令空气在飞机机翼下流过产生升力，飞机便可停止下坠，但当时机长对这些建议完全没有回应。可能是机长当时已方寸大乱，又或是机长认为他有相当多的驾驶 757 的经验，自尊心令他忽视只有 75 小时驾驶 757 经验的资历浅的副驾驶的建议。无论如何，他们损失了太多高度无法挽回飞机，最终导致 189 人死亡。

After the crash, the FAA asked Boeing to improve the 757's design by adding a warning that the pilot's and co-pilot's airspeed gauges were different. At the same time, Boeing is incorporating the crash into its pilot training program.

空难发生后，FAA 要求波音改进 757 的设计，增加了驾驶员空速表和副驾驶员空速表不一致的告警。同时，波音将这次空难纳入飞行员培训项目。

2.3　Reason Model
2.3　Reason 模型

The Swiss Cheese model of accident causation, originally proposed by James Reason, likens human system defenses to a series of slices of randomly-holed Swiss Cheese arranged vertically and parallel to each other with gaps in-between each slice.

瑞士奶酪模型是针对事故原因的，最初由 James Reason 提出，又称 Reason 模型。将防御比作一系列随机穿孔的瑞士奶酪片，这些瑞士奶酪片垂直平行排列，每片之间有间隙。

Reason Model hypothesizes that most accidents can be traced to one or more of four levels of failure: organizational influences, unsafe supervision, preconditions for unsafe acts, and the unsafe acts themselves.

Reason 模型假设大多数事故都可以追溯到四个级别的故障中的一个或多个：组织影响、不安全监督、不安全行为的前提条件和不安全行为本身。

In the Swiss Cheese model, an organization's defenses against failure are modelled as a series of barriers, represented as slices of the cheese. The holes in the cheese slices represent individual weaknesses in individual parts of the system, and are continually varying in size and position in all slices. The system as a whole produces failure when holes in all of the slices momentarily align, permitting "a trajectory of accident opportunity", so that a hazard passes through holes in all of the defenses, leading to an accident, as shown in Figure 2-2.

在“瑞士奶酪”模式中，一个组织对失败的防御被建模为一系列的壁垒，以奶酪片的形式表现出来。奶酪切片上的孔代表了系统各个部分的个别弱点，并且在所有切片上的大小和位置不断变化。整个系统会发生故障，当所有的碎片上的洞瞬间对齐，“事故的轨迹”穿过所有防御工事上的洞，导致事故发生，如图 2-2 所示。

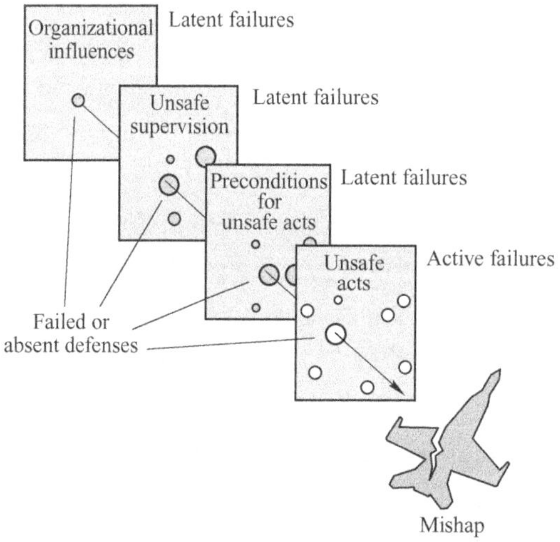

Figure 2-2　Reason model

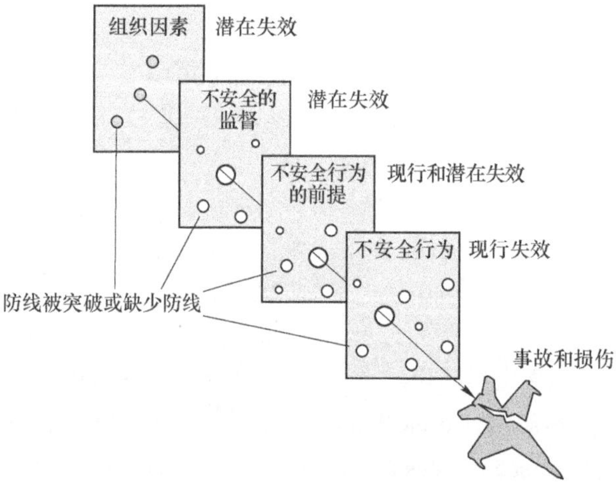

图 2-2　Reason 模型

2.4　Murphy's Law
2.4　墨菲定律

Murphy's Law ("If anything can go wrong, it will") was born at Edwards Air Force Base in 1949 at North Base. It was named after. Edward A. Murphy, an engineer working on Air Force Project MX981。

墨菲定律指出"凡是可能出错的都会出错"，它是由当时参与美国空军高速载人工具火箭雪橇 MX981 发展计划的工程师爱德华·A. 墨菲提出的。

Flight Training Files
飞行训练档案

Case
案例

Xiao Ming had a bad time recently. The instructor failed his lessons several times for various reasons, and the base manager gave him a few days'leave to adjust himself. At this time, there was a rumor among the students that Xiao Ming was going to be terminated. Xiao Ming not only lay sullenly in bed all day, eating and drinking nothing, but also lost enthusiasm for learning. What should Xiao Ming do now? What should you do if you were his classmate?

小明最近过得很糟糕，连续几节课被教员以各种各样的理由“挂”了，基地经理给了他几天假让他好好调整。此时同学们中有风言风语传出小明即将被退训的消息。小明整天躺在床上闷闷不乐，不但不吃不喝，还失去了对学习的热情。小明此时应该怎么办？如果你是小明的同学，你应该怎么办？

Briefing
讲评

When facing pressure, Xiao Ming should adjust himself. He can talk to his classmates, instructors, teachers and family to relieve stress. He can get to those'good students'for flying techniques, then reinforce his SOP. It's normal to face problems during the flying training, we should face the difficulty breaking through ourselves to turn the corner. As a classmate, you can understand the difficulties better, when someone is performing bad, try to give him some help, getting him out of the terrible situation.

在面对压力时，小明应该调整好心态，可以通过与同学、教员、学校老师或家人的沟通缓解压力。可以向飞得好的同学请教飞行技巧，自己抽时间巩固飞行标准程序。学飞生涯中遇到坎坷很正常，应该正视困难突破自我才能转危为安。作为同学，更应对飞行中的坎坷深有体会，在同学或朋友遇到困难或低谷时，多给予他鼓励，陪他一起走过困难的时光。

Unit 2
Crew Communication

第 2 篇　机组沟通与交流

Lead-in
课程导入

On January 25th of 1990, Avianca flight 052 En-route from Bogota, Columbia to John F. Kennedy International Airport (JFK) in New York, crash landed 24km from the airport due to starvation of fuel. Upon arrival of JKF airspace, the conditions of climate were degrading as time went by. Upon the third ***holding point*** the crew informed ***Air Traffic Control*** they will not be able to hold for no more that 5 minutes and will not have sufficient fuel to land at the alternate airport in Boston. Therefore, Avianca 052 continued its flight towards JFK, however upon an ***Instrument landing system (ILS)*** descend, the crew could not maintain a stabilised approach or profile due to the strong wind shear. ***Visibility*** was a great concern too and as a result, a ***go ground*** was required. Upon second attempt on approach about 32km from the airport, flight 052 crew had realised that they were closer to the end of their reserve fuels, immediately a radio call was made to Air traffic Controllers advised that "We're running out of fuel, sir", however tower requested in reply to climb. Momentary after the radio call, all four engines flamed out and electrical power was lost and the aircraft descended down rapidly into the vicinity of a small wealthy village, 24km from the Airfield and crashed, with no fire. 73 passengers and crew died with 85 injured.

1990 年 1 月 25 日，从哥伦比亚波哥大飞往纽约肯尼迪国际机场（JFK）的哥伦比亚 052 号航班在离机场 24 千米的地方因燃料耗尽坠毁。抵达肯尼迪机场空域后，随着时间的推移，气候条件越来越差。在等待航线飞了三圈之后，机组人员通知空中交通管制他们没有足够的燃油，剩余的燃油只能维持 5 分钟，无法在波士顿机场备降。因此，哥伦比亚 052 号航班机继续飞往肯尼迪机场，并使用仪表着陆系统（ILS）下降高度，当时遭遇了强烈的风切变，导致机组人员无法保持稳定进近。同时，能见度低，机组需要复飞。机组在距离机场 32 千米处试图进行第二次着陆，此时他们已经意识到燃油即将耗尽，立即用无线电呼叫了空中交通管制员“管制，我们即将耗尽燃料”，塔台回复让飞机爬升。随即，4 个引擎全部熄火，飞机失去了电源系统，并快速降落到距离机场 24 千米的小村庄附近，飞机坠毁，没有起火。机上共有 73 名乘客和机组人员死亡，85 人受伤。

First officer Mauricio Klotz repeatedly reported to air traffic control that the machine was running out of fuel, but did not explicitly state that it was an emergency. In landing phase, Klotz was instructed several times by Captain Caviedes to explain an air emergency. Klotz did not follow this instruction, but merely repeated to air traffic control that the fuel was running low; however, he claimed to Caviedes that he had declared an air emergency. At 20: 44: 43, while holding at CAMRN, the New York (NY) ARTCC radar controller advised AVA052 to expect further clearance (EFC) at 21: 05. The flight had previously been issued EFC times of 2030 and 2039. The first officer responded, " ... ah well I think we need priority ... ".

副驾驶毛里西奥·克鲁兹多次向空中交通管制中心报告，飞机燃料即将耗尽，但并没有明确宣布紧急情况。在着陆阶段，机长卡维德多次给予克鲁兹指令，令其向管制宣布飞机进入紧急情况。克鲁兹没有遵照这一指示，只是向空中交通管制人员重复说，燃料快用完了；然而，他对卡维德说，他已经宣布了空中紧急情况。20：44：43，在 CAMRN 等待时，纽约 ARTCC 雷达管制员告知机组会在 21：05 给出下一步指令。副驾回答说：“……我认为我们需要优先权……”。

The National Transportation Safety Board determines that the probable cause of this accident was the failure of the flight crew to adequately manage the airplane's fuel load, and their failure to communicate an emergency fuel situation to air traffic control before fuel exhaustion occurred. Also contributing to the accident was inadequate traffic flow management by the FAA and the lack of standardized understandable terminology for pilots and controllers for ***minimum and emergency fuel*** states. The Safety Board also determines that ***windshear***, crew ***fatigue*** and stress were factors that led to the unsuccessful completion of the first approach and thus contributed to the accident.

美国国家运输安全委员会认定，这起事故的可能原因是机组人员未能充分管理飞机的燃油负载，以及他们未能在燃油耗尽之前向空中交通管制部门通报紧急燃油情况。造成事故的一个原因是美国联邦航空局的交通流量管理不到位，以及飞行员和管制员并不理解在最低和紧急燃料状态时标准的陆空通话术语。风切变、机组疲劳和压力是导致第一次着陆失败的因素，从而导致了事故的发生。

Key words

关键词

holding point	等待点
Air Traffic Control	空中交通管制
Instrument landing system（ILS）	仪表着陆系统
visibility	能见度
go ground	复飞
priority	优先权
minimum fuel	最低燃油量
emergency fuel	紧急燃油量
windshear	风切变
fatigue	疲劳

Discussion

讨论

（1）Why did the co-pilot use "priority" instead of "emergency" in your opinion?

（1）你认为副驾驶在通话中没有使用“紧急”而是使用了“优先”的原因是什么？

（2）What is the standard radio telephony phrase in this situation?

（2）在这种情况下，陆空通话的标准表达是什么？

Advanced thinking

高阶思维

Please use SHEL model to analysis this accident.

请使用 SHEL 模型分析这起事故。

S

H

E

L

Lesson 3　Basic Concepts
第 3 课　基本概念

3.1　What is Crew Communication
3.1　什么是机组交流

Communication is the process of exchanging information, thoughts and emotions in a timely manner that is pleasant and easy to understand.

交流是以令人愉快和易于理解的方式及时交换信息、思维与情感的过程。

The scope of communication is very wide. The main objects of a pilot's communication during flight include: communication with air traffic controllers, communication with other aircraft, communication with cabin attendants, communication with passengers, communication with the aircraft itself and communication with ground personnel.

交流的范围很广泛，一个飞行员在飞行过程中交流的对象主要包括：与空中交通管制员之间的交流，与其他飞机的交流，与客舱乘务员的交流，与乘客之间的交流，与飞机本身的交流以及与地面人员的交流。

3.2　Categories of Communication
3.2　交流的分类

There is one-way communication, e.g., from cockpit instruments to the pilot; and there is two-way communication, which also called interpersonal communication, this includes communication between individuals on the flight deck, in the cabin, and anyone involved in the operation.

交流中有单向的，例如，驾驶舱仪表与飞行员之间；有双向的，也叫人际沟通，这包括飞行甲板上的个人之间的沟通、客舱内的沟通以及所有参与操作的人之间的沟通。

Crew communication has two types: verbal, nonverbal.

交流分为言语交流和非言语交流。

3.2.1　Verbal Communication
3.2.1　言语交流

Verbal communication can be divided into written communication, that is, information exchange with the help of written materials. The crew receives various forms of written information during flight, such as checklists, standard operating procedures, navigational notices, and so on. The other is oral communication, which refers to the communication with the help of spoken language. Oral communication is the most common form of communication in group communication.

言语交流包括书面交流，即借助书面文字材料实现的信息交流。机组成员在飞行过程中会接收到各种形式的书面信息，如检查单、标准操作程序、航行通告等。此外，言语交流也包括口头交流，是指借助口语语言实现的交流，口头交流是机组交流中最经常的交流形式。

Besides, verbal communication can be categorized into standard operation procedure communication, management communication and non-related communication. The particularity of flight crew requires more standardized and clear verbal communication in the cockpit, namely standard operation procedure communication. Management communication relates to management beyond standard operation procedures. It is particularly necessary to strengthen administrative unit communication under abnormal conditions. Non-related communication refers to communication that is not directly related to flight activities and situations.

言语交流被分为标准操作程序交流、管理性交流与无关交流等三种类别。飞行机组工作的特殊性要求机组成员在驾驶舱中更多地使用标准化的、清晰的言语交流方式，即标准操作程序交流。管理性交流与标准操作程序以外的管理有关。在非正常情况下特别需要加强管理性的机组交流。无关交流是指与飞行活动和情景没有直接关系的交流。

Verbal communication or speech is the most common communication medium used in an aircraft or in the aviation industry. It is used by the cabin crew, aircraft technicians, pilots, and flight attendants who use this medium to take care and communicate with the passengers. Also, this type of communication reduces the misunderstanding and miscommunication when it comes to giving a job order or information.

在飞机驾驶舱或航空产业中，口头交流或言语交流是最常见的交流媒介。机组人员、飞机技术人员、飞行员和空乘人员都使用这一媒介来照顾和与乘客沟通。这种沟通方式可以减少在下达工作指令或提供信息时的误解。

The Sterile Cockpit Rule is an FAA regulation requiring pilots to refrain from non-essential activities during critical phases of flight, normally below 10000 feet. The FAA imposed the rule in 1981 after reviewing a series of accidents that were caused by flight crews who were distracted from their flying duties by engaging in non-essential conversations and activities during critical parts of the flight, as shown in Figure 3-1.

美国联邦航空管理局（FAA）有一项“静默驾驶舱”的规定，要求飞行员在飞行关键阶段（通常在10000英尺以下）避免进行非必要活动。1981年，美国联邦航空局在审查了一系列事故后实施了这一规定，他们发现很多事故是由机组人员在飞行关键阶段进行非必要的谈话和活动，从而导致他们在执行飞行任务时分心，如图3-1所示。

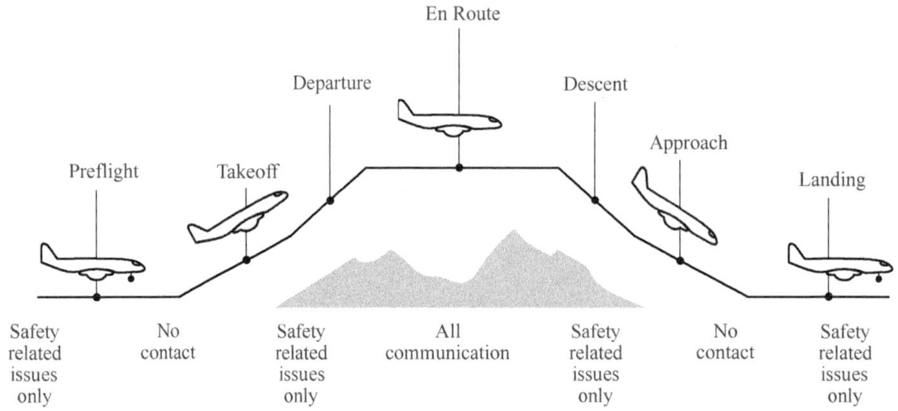

Figure 3-1 Sterile cockpit rule

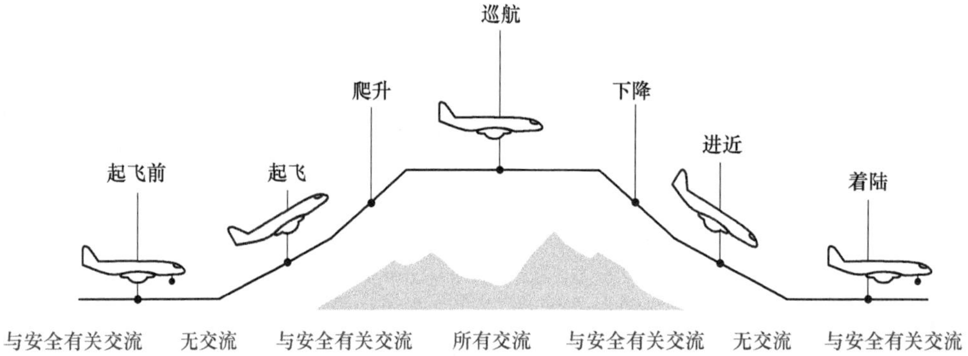

图 3-1 静默驾驶舱

扫一扫查看彩图

3. 2. 2 Non-verbal, such as Body Language

3. 2. 2 非言语交流，如肢体语言

Hand signals from the ground to the cockpit, between crewmembers during certain routine operations, or between cabin crew and passengers during or after an encounter with clear air turbulence, as shown in Figure 3-2.

地面人员向驾驶舱发出的手势，在某些常规操作中机组人员之间的手势，或在遇到晴空乱流时或之后，客舱机组人员与乘客之间的手势，如图 3-2 所示。

Nonverbal communication is important in every person-to-person situation. It has two major kinds-body language and physical appearance.

在人际交往中，非言语交流发挥着重要作用。它有两种主要类型——肢体语言和表情。

Figure 3-2　Ground marshalling signals
图 3-2　机场地面人员手势

扫一扫查看彩图

Lesson 4 Three Communication Models
第4课 三种交流模式

4.1 The Shannon & Weaver Model
4.1 Shannon & Weaver 模式

Shannon and Weaver (1949) introduced a simple communication model that still serves as a reference for technical applications. This simple, linear model was developed as part of a mathematical theory of communication.

Shannon 和 Weaver 介绍了一种简单的交流模式，这一模式至今仍然作为一种参考模式广泛运用于技术应用。这种简单、线性的模式被发展成了交流的数学理论中的一部分。

This model states that all communication must include six elements: a source, an encoder, a message, a channel, a decoder and a receiver. When, for instance, you use the cockpit radio, you speak, the radio turns the sound waves into VHF waves and those waves are turned back into sound waves by the radio at the other end of the line, as shown in Figure 4-1.

该模式认为所有的交流都包括6个元素：交流源、编码器、信息、通道、解码器以及接收者。例如，驾驶舱无线电的使用包括飞行员讲话、无线电将其声波转换为甚高频、甚高频在线的另一端又被无线电转换成声波，如图4-1所示。

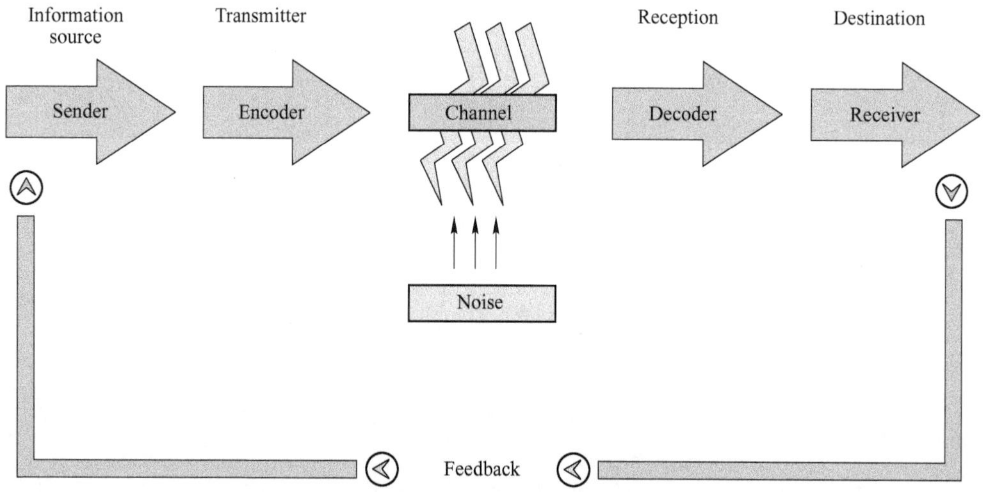

Figure 4-1 Shannon-Weaver's model of communication

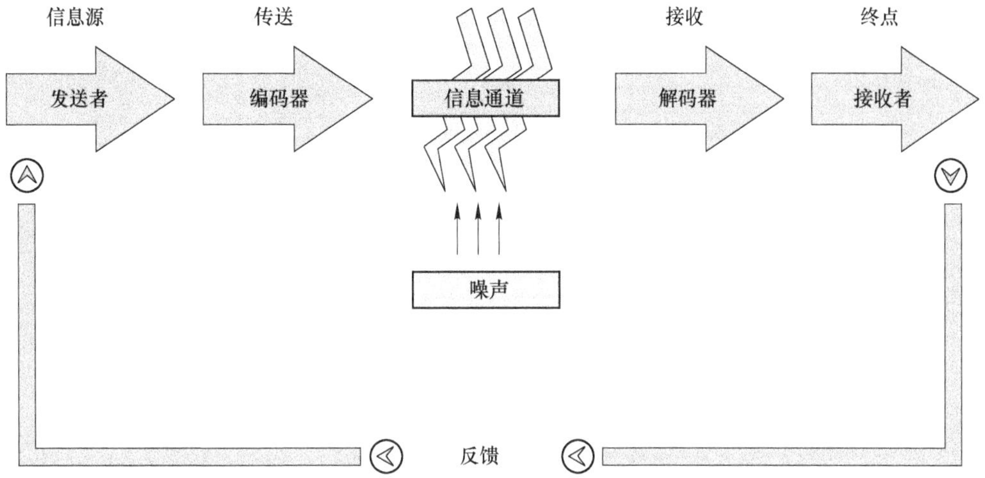

图 4-1　Shannon-Weaver 交流模型

The emphasis here is on the transmission and reception of information, so this model is often referred to as an " information model" of communication. Is that transfer useful? Are there limitations? Can human communication be reduced solely to an exchange of information?

该模式在这里所强调的信息的传递与接收，又被称为“信息模式”。这样的传送方式有用吗？有什么限制？人类的交流能不能被简化成只是一种信息的交换呢？

4.2　The Berlo Model
4.2　Berlo 模式

Berlo (1960) has proposed a different approach more suitable to tackle the complexity of human communication. His primary interest was on dyadic, also called one to one communication, looking for non technical conditions needed for the communication success or fidelity.

1960 年，Berlo 提出了另一种更适合解释人类交流复杂性的方法。他的研究主要集中在双向交流上，也被称之为一对一交流，他寻求一种促成成功交流的非技术性条件。

In this perspective, the success of communication is not defined only in terms of similarity between the transmitted and the received messages, as it was the case in the Shannon and Weaver model. On the contrary, Berlo places great emphasis on the role of the relationship between the two actors as a condition of success or failure.

从这点出发，我们对交流成功的定义就不能像是在 Shannon & Weaver 模式中那样，只将其界定为发送与接收信息。相反，Berlo 特别强调了交流双方之间的关系对交流成功或失败所起的作用。

For this purpose, he introduced a sociologically influenced model that identifies four components of communication: source, message, channel, and receiver, each of these components featuring several qualities or modes. For instance, the source and the receiver are characterized by their communication skills, knowledge, social system, culture and attitudes, as shown in Figure 4-2.

为此，他引入了受社会学影响的模式。该模式将交流分为 4 个组成部分：发送者、信息、通道及接收者，每一组成部分都有其特质。以信源（发送者）为例，其特征：传播技术、态度、知识、社会系统、文化，如图 4-2 所示。

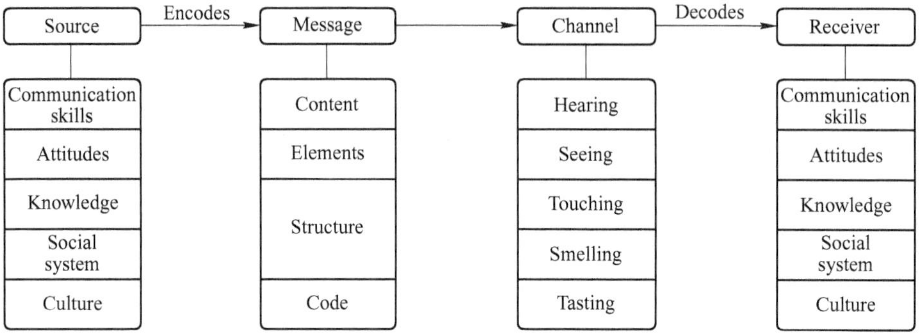

Figure 4-2　Berlo's SMCR model of communication

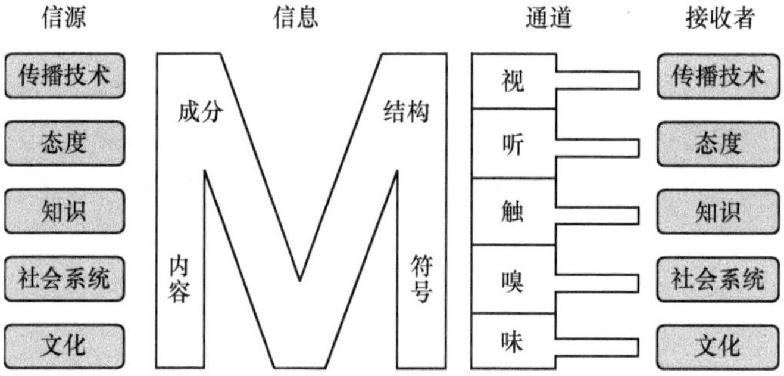

图 4-2　Berlo 模式

4.3　The Context Model
4.3　语境模式

The context model is another attempt to enrich Shannon-Weaver's linear model of communication. It states that success in communication depending on two basic aspects: the form and the meaning.

另一种试图完善 Shannon-Weaver 交流线性模型的是语境模式。语境模式认为，交流的成功取决于两个非常基本的方面：形式和含义。

The transmitter and the receiver must speak a common language. Although this is essential, it is far from being enough. The sentences must be correctly formed and, if possible, unambiguous. Moreover, gestures and attitudes may duplicate speech either attenuate or accentuate its context. This message to be decoded is the sum of all verbal and non-verbal expression, as shown in Figure 4-3.

发送者和接收者必须使用同一种语言。这是必要条件，仅仅使用同种语言还远远不够。交流语句必须使用正确的形式表达出来，尽可能做到没有歧义。此外，手势和态度能代替言语，他们可以削弱或是加强言语内容。解码信息包括其语言表达及非语言表达的总和，如图 4-3 所示。

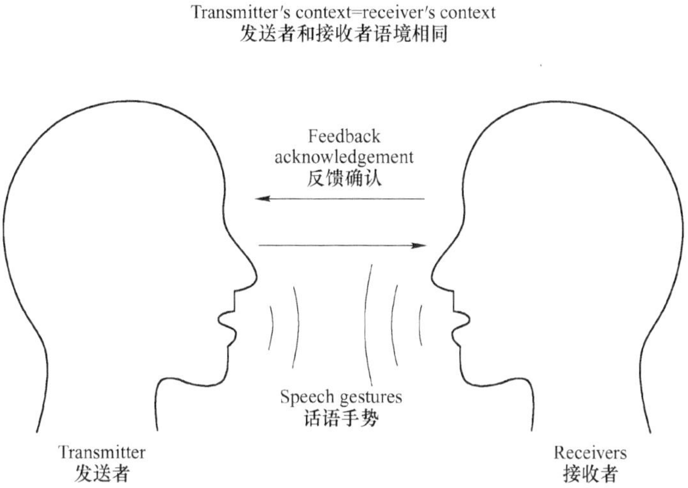

Figure 4-3　Common context makes communication possible
图 4-3　相同的语境让交流通畅

However, the meaning of what is said does not solely depend on form. It also depends on the transimitter's and the receiver's contexts. Within different context, the same phrase can have very different meanings. If crew members don't have the same context, communication will consist of a series of misunderstandings, as shown in Figure 4-4.

然而交流中所表达的含义并不只取决于形式，它还取决于发送者与接收者的交流语境。在不同的语境中，同一短语可能有不同的含义。如果机组成员之间没有相同的语境，交流中就会产生一系列的误解，如图 4-4 所示。

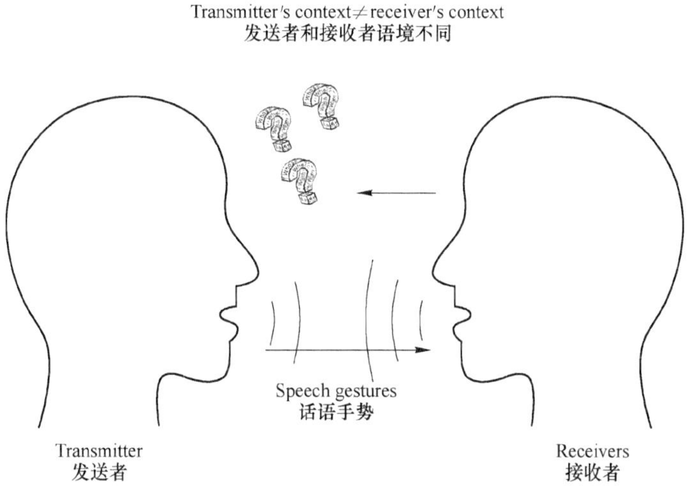

Figure 4-4　Different contexts make communication impossible
图 4-4　不同的语境无法通畅交流

4.4　Case study
4.4　案例分析

A routine IFR approach. The weather was bad and the ceiling was low.
一次常规的仪表飞行进近。天气不好，云很低。

1000ft above minima
距离最低高度 1000 英尺

The crew extended flaps 1 then flaps 2. The captain noticed that the first officer was moving his hand to the ceiling panel to operate a system.

副驾驶正在头顶板上操作一个系统，机长被他的动作吸引，同时机组放出襟翼 1 和 2。

（1）Captain："Generator 1 fault? Leave it, we're almost there..."
（1）机长："一号发电机失效了吗？不要管他，我们就快到了……"

800 feet
800 英尺

（2）First Officer："No, not exactly..."
（2）副驾驶："不是，不太确定……"
（3）Captain："What do you mean?"
（3）机长："什么意思？"

600 feet
600 英尺

（4）First Officer："Generator 1 has not really failed..."
（4）副驾驶："一号发电机不是真的失效了"。
（5）Captain："But is the voltage OK now?"
（5）机长："电压正常吗？"

400 feet
400 英尺

（6）First Officer："Yes. Nothing serious, Jim, just a small voltage surge. Take care, we're nearly there."
（6）副驾驶："嗯，问题不大，电压有点摆动，小心，我们快到了。"
（7）Captain："OK, flaps full."
（7）机长："好的，全襟翼。"
When the flaps were fully extended, the landing gear horn sounded.
当襟翼全部放出时，起落架警告响起。

100 feet
100 英尺

The landing gear was lowered at the last moment.
起落架在最后关头放出。

This dialogue during an approach illustrates several typical pitfalls in verbal communication. The captain interrupts his approach context briefly（1）to attend to the situation implied by his first officer. The captain then attempts to divert the first officer back to his own context（2）, ignore the problem and continue the approach.

在这段进近中的通话，列举了言语交流中几种常见的交流陷阱。机长中断自己的进近语境（1），转而去关注副驾驶操作的新语境。接着，机长试图把副驾驶拉回到自己的进近语境中来（2），告知副驾驶不要管那个故障，继续进近。

The first officer is in a failure context and does not initially understand that he should ignore it. On the contrary, he thinks that he should continue with his analysis. He replies with a phrase（2）that serves to keep the captain's attention on their communication. The captain then leaves his approach context（3）in favour of his first officer's failure context in order to dialogue with him concerning the problem. Again, the first officer's answer（4）serves to retain the captain's attention by telling him that an analysis result is imminent. Fortunately, the situation is corrected at the last moment when the first officer redirects the captain back to the approach context（6）.

副驾驶起初并没有理解机长的意思，反而专注于故障分析，他回答了（2）的语句，让机长的注意力停留在副驾驶的故障语境中。接着，机长离开自己的进近语境（3），转向了副驾驶的故障语境，和副驾驶对话。副驾驶的回答（4）引起了机长的注意，他汇报了自己故障分析的结果。幸运的是，到了最后一刻，副驾驶把机长又带回到进近语境（6）。

Consequently, in order to understand a message, it is necessary to shift one's context and thus, at least temporarily, abandon one's previous context. It is therefore essential for a sender to take into account his or her receiver's activity before attempting to communicate with him and to disturb him as little as possible. The contrary is also true: take great care in accepting interruptions when you yourself are carrying out a task.

因此，想要理解信息，必须转换语境，至少要先放下上一个的语境。信息发送者在他或她试图与接收者交流之前，应该考虑对方正在进行的活动，并尽可以不去打断对方的语境。这一点非常重要，反之，当你进行信息传递的任务时，也要注意到别人对你的干扰。

Lesson 5　Communication Barriers
第 5 课　交流障碍

5.1　Internal Barriers and External Barriers
5.1　内部障碍和外部障碍

Communication barrier is anything that interferes with or hinders communication and impairs it. They are present throughout the communication process and have the potential to influence how we send, receive and respond to information at any time. Communication barrier can exist within two sides, or they can come from outside of us.

交流障碍是干扰或是阻碍交流以及削弱交流的一切事件。它们存在于交流过程的始终，并随时有可能影响我们的信息发送、接收以及反馈。障碍可以存在于交流双发的内部，也可能来自我们的外部。

External barriers include various media that affect communication and collaboration, such as sound, light, temperature, workload, etc.

外部障碍包括影响交流、协作的各种媒介，如声、光、温度、工作负荷等。

Internal barriers include factors that influence communication brought in by participants in communication. They affect how information is encoded, how it is sent, how it is interpreted, and so on. Internal barriers include prejudice, attitude, life experience, self-awareness, body language, etc.

内部障碍包括交流的参与者所带入的影响交流的因素。它们影响信息的编码、信息的发送方式、信息的解释方式等。内部障碍包括偏见、态度、生活阅历、自我意识、身体语言等。

5.2　Radio Telephony Errors
5.2　陆空通话差错

At present, Chinese and foreign scholars have carried out relevant studies on the error of land-air communication. Abroad, based on 12373 ASRS reports (1978-1980), Billings et al. found that errors in air and land voice communication between controller and pilot were one of the main causes of aviation insecurity incidents. In 1989, Golaszewski et al. first studied the impact of pilot repetition errors on flight safety, and defined and classified the repetition errors. Cohen et al. studied the problem of pilot recitation within the scope of tower control, approach control and regional control respectively. Morrow pointed out that the command length and timing of air-to-land communication had a certain influence on pilot recitation performance. In 2006, Prinzo et al. first conducted a quantitative analysis on the influence of command complexity, command length, pilot language ability and other factors on pilot repetition errors based on about 100 hours of real land and air call recordings from us terminal approach control and air route control units. Nitta et al. studied the influence of the speed of speech on the comprehension of pilots when American controllers were talking with non-native English speakers.

目前，国内外学者对陆空通话差错进行了相关研究。在国外，根据 12373 份 ASRS 报告（1978~1980 年），Billings 等人发现管制员和飞行员之间的空中和地面通信错误是航空不安全事件的主要原因之一。1989 年，Golaszewski 等人首次研究了飞行员复诵误差对飞行安全的影响，并对复诵误差进行了定义和分类。Cohen 等人分别在塔台控制、进近控制和区域控制范围内研究了飞行员背诵问题。Morrow 指出，陆空通话指令长度和发话时机对飞行员复诵表现有一定影响。2006 年，Prinzo 等人首先基于美国终端进近管制和航路管制单位的约 100 小时实况真实陆空通话录音，对指令复杂性、指令长度、飞行员语言能力等因素对飞行员复诵错误的影响进行了定量分析。NITTA 等人研究了当美国空管人员与非英语母语飞行员通话时，语速对飞行员理解能力的影响。

In China, in 1996, Liu Lan and others began to pay attention to the procedures, expressions and errors of land-air communication. In 2000, Huo Zhiqin first began to study the repetition errors of pilots in domestic land-air communication, and analyzed the types and influencing factors of repetition errors. Pan Weijun et al. studied the call errors in tower control, approach control and area control respectively. Wang Yanqing et al. analyzed the causes of pilots'performance and errors in air-to-land communication from the perspective of psychological cognition. Liu Jixin et al. studied the cognitive behavior and cognitive function in the process of air-ground communication between controllers and pilots. Sun Ruishan et al. analyzed the influence of the voice characteristics of controllers'land-air calls on controllers'fatigue warning and pilots'repetition errors.

在中国，从 1996 年开始，刘兰等人开始关注陆空通话的程序、表达方式和错误。2000 年，霍志勤首先开始研究国内陆空通话中飞行员的复诵错误，分析了复诵错误的类型和影响因素。潘伟军等分别研究了塔台控制、进近控制和区域控制中的发话误差。王燕青等从心理认知角度分析了飞行员在陆空通话中表现和失误的原因。刘继新等人研究了管制员与飞行员空对地通信过程中的认知行为和认知功能。孙瑞山等分析了管制员地空呼叫语音特性对管制员疲劳预警和飞行员陆空通复诵错误的影响。

Shang Liqin (2021) collected voice data of 46.2 hours of international flight calls across different regions from airlines, processed the data with text analysis method and obtained 2,535 calls. Meanwhile, questionnaire survey and in-depth interview were conducted for relevant pilots. Five factor sets of call characteristics, pilot characteristics, controller characteristics, airspace characteristics and frequency interference were proposed. Finally, a Logistic model was established to quantitatively analyze the influencing factors of pilot repetition errors in different regions. The results showed that: Pilots' language ability and the use of standard terms were significantly correlated with the level of repetition errors in each region; Radio frequency interference (Asia, North America, Europe), communication complexity (Asia, Europe), controller accent (Asia), controller speed (North America) were significantly correlated with the level of pilot repetition error.

尚立琴（2021）从航空公司采集跨越不同区域的 46. 2 小时国际航班通话语音数据，采用文字记录分析法对数据进行处理，获取 2535 句通话，同时针对相关飞行员实施问卷调查和深度访谈，提出通话特征、飞行员特点、管制员特点、空域特点和频率干扰 5 个维度的因素集，最后建立 Logistic 模型分区域定量分析飞行员复诵差错的影响因素。结果表明：飞行员语言能力、是否使用标准通话术语在各区域均与飞行员复诵差错水平呈现显著相关；无线电频率干扰（亚洲、北美、欧洲）、通话复杂程度（亚洲、欧洲）、管制员口音（亚洲）、管制员语速（北美）与飞行员复诵差错水平呈现显著相关。

5. 3　Case Study
5. 3　案例分析

Tenerife Disaster
特内里费岛空难

On March 27th, 1977, the day of the accident, neither aircraft should have been in Tenerife in the first place. Indeed, both of them had been bound for the neighboring island of Gran Canaria. However, a terrorist incident at Gran Canaria Airport (LPA) forced several inbound aircraft to divert to Tenerife Los Rodeos Airpor.

1977 年 3 月 27 日，两架飞机本来都不应该出现在特内里费岛。事实上，这两架飞机都是飞往邻近的大卡纳利亚岛的。然而，在大卡纳利亚机场（LPA）发生的恐怖事件迫使几架入境飞机备降特内里费岛的洛斯罗迪奥斯机场。

The Pan Am 747-100 had come from Los Angeles International (LAX) via New York JFK, with the KLM 747-200 arriving from Amsterdam Schipol (AMS) . Congestion at the comparatively small airport forced planes to park on the taxiway. This meant that, by the time Gran Canaria Airport reopened, the Pan Am aircraft was stuck behind the KLM jumbo, which was refueling.

泛美航空公司的 747-100 从洛杉矶国际机场起飞，经停纽约肯尼迪机场抵达洛斯罗迪奥斯机场，荷兰皇家航空公司的 747-200 从阿姆斯特丹史基浦机场起飞抵达洛斯罗迪奥斯机场。飞机的到来使得这个相对较小的机场出现拥堵，迫使大量飞机停在滑行道上。这意味着，当大卡纳利亚机场宣布重新开放时，泛美航空公司的飞机排在了正在加油的荷航客机后面。

While the diverted aircraft had been on the ground, a thick fog had enveloped the airport.

当这些改航的飞机降落在跑道上时，浓雾笼罩了机场。

Eventually, air traffic control (ATC) instructed the KLM 747 to taxi down the runway, with Pan Am's jumbo following shortly afterward. The former was told to turn around at the end of the strip to make its departure, with the latter was told to exit the runway at the third turnoff.

最终，空中交通管制（ATC）命令 KLM 747 反向滑行至跑道头，泛美航空的 747 紧随其后。前者在跑道尽头掉头离开跑道，后者则被告知在第三个脱离道离开跑道。

A diagram depicting Tenerife North Airport and the two aircraft's paths in Figure 5-1.

图 5-1 中画出了特内里费北机场和两架飞机的滑行路线。

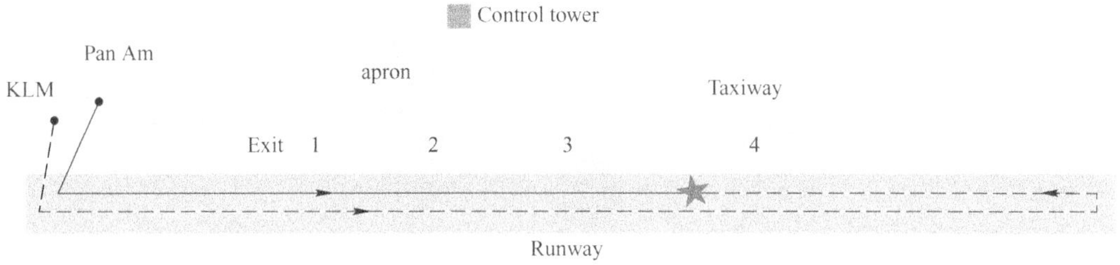

Figure 5-1　Tenerife disaster

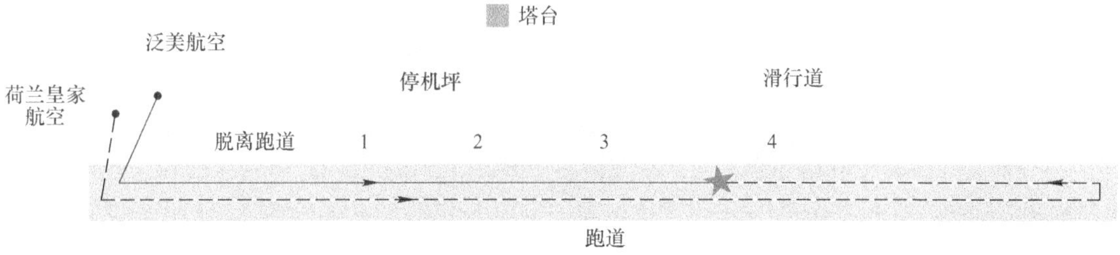

图 5-1　特内里费岛空难

扫一扫查看彩图

However, the Pan Am crew was unfamiliar with the airport, and struggled to locate the exit among the fog. This led to them missing it altogether and continuing down the runway. In any case, it is thought that the acute angle, as seen above, would have been too tight a turn for the large aircraft to make.

然而，泛美航空的机组人员对机场并不熟悉，在大雾中很难找到第三个脱离道。这导致他们完全错过了它，继续沿着跑道前进。飞行员认为，对于 747 这样的大型客机而言，在第三个脱离道转弯的大角度很难操作。

Meanwhile, the KLM 747 had made its turn at the end of the runway, and was lined up ready for departure. The KLM crew read back their ATC clearance detailing the route out of Tenerife, concluding with the phrase "we are now at takeoff," meaning that they were ready to depart. The tower responded, "okay, stand by for takeoff; I will call you."

与此同时，荷兰皇家航空公司的 747 飞机已经在跑道的尽头调头，排队等候起飞。荷兰皇家航空的机组人员复诵了管制许可，详细说明了离开特内里费岛的航路，最后说了一句“we are now at takeoff”，意思是他们已经准备好出发了。塔台回答说：“好的，稍等起飞；我一会叫你。”

However, a simultaneous radio message from the Pan Am aircraft caused interference on the frequency. This meant that the KLM crew did not hear all of the tower's message, and began their takeoff roll due to the use of "okay" having seemingly implied permission to depart.

然而，泛美航空的飞行员同时也在使用无线电信息，对通信造成了频率干扰，导致荷兰皇家航空公司的机组人员没有把塔台的指令听完整，就开始滑跑，他们认为塔台说的

“好的” 意味着允许起飞。

Tragically, the interference also meant that the KLM crew could not hear the Pan Am crew's transmission of "we're still taxiing down the runway. " Despite last-minute attempts to vacate the landing strip by the Pan Am 747, and from the KLM crew to lift their's into the air, the jumbos collided near the runway's fourth exit.

不幸的是，此时无线电的干扰也意味着荷兰皇家航空公司的机组人员听不到泛美航空公司机组人员发出的“我们仍在跑道上滑行” 的通话。尽管泛美航空公司的 747 客机和荷兰皇家航空公司的机组人员在最后一刻都试图离开跑道，并将飞机升到空中，但这两架大型客机还是在第四条脱离道附近相撞。

Overall, 583 passengers and crew onboard the two planes lost their lives in the fiery collision. There were just 61 survivors, all of whom had been onboard the Pan Am 747. KLM eventually admitted primary responsibility in the accident, due to its crew having begun their takeoff roll without permission. Since the crash, standardized phrases have become a crucial part of ATC communications, to ensure that such deadly confusion does not occur again.

两架飞机在剧烈碰撞中总共有 583 名乘客和机组人员丧生，泛美航空有 61 名幸存者。荷航最终宣称对这起事故负有主要责任，因为机组人员在未经允许的情况下开始滑跑。自飞机失事以来，标准化的陆空通话已成为空中交通管制通信的一个关键部分，以确保这种致命的混乱不会再次发生。

5.4　How to Improve Crew Communication Skill
5.4　如何提高机组交流技能

While the basic process of communication or skill is to send and receive and feedback information, we also need to develop special skill of communication in order to effectively completed the communication process and the rational use of these basic communication. They are inquiry and response, advice, and briefing and evaluation, as shown in Table 5-1.

虽然交流的基本过程或者技能是发送和接收以及反馈信息，但为了有效地完成这些交流过程和合理使用这些基本的交流技能，我们还需要在这些基本技能的基础上发展有利于机组交流的一些特殊技能，这就是质询与反应、劝告、简述与讲评，见表 5-1。

Table 5-1　Communication skills

表 5-1　交流技能

Inquiry and Response	质询与反应
Ask for the right questions	要求正确的提问
Collect and validate data	收集和验证数据
Inquire promptly and update information constantly	及时质询，不断地更新信息
Test accuracy	检验准确性
Identify the most serious threats	识别出最严重的威胁
Comment on the inquiry	对质询做出评价
Take safe action	采取稳妥的行动

Continued Table5-1

续表 5-1

Advice	劝告
State your opinion directly Express your concerns and concerns Get other people's opinions	直接地陈述意见 表达自己的关心和担忧 征求其他人的意见
Briefing	简述
Two-way Realistic flight problems are involved in the current scenario The closed-loop system	双向进行 针对当前情景，涉及现实的飞行问题 闭环系统
Evaluation	讲评
Timely evaluation Offer constructive comments Lay the foundation for further ensuring flight safety	及时讲评 提出建设性的意见 为进一步确保飞行安全奠定基础

Here are some practical rules to improve crew communication and maintain a good grasp of situation.

以下是一些可以提高飞行员的沟通能力、保持较好情景意识的实用规则。

(1) Use a professional language.

(1) 使用专业的语言。

Speak clearly, concisely and unambiguously. Always acknowledge messages received. Do not hesitate to ask for the message to be repeated if you have any doubt.

交流时使用的语言要清楚、简明、明确。收到的消息总是可以做到给予确认。如果你有任何疑问，请不要犹豫，要求对方重复一次。

(2) Call outs.

(2) 喊话。

The standard announcement of modes, situations, etc. are a guarantee that the whole crew share the same image of the situation.

标准喊话可以确保机组处于同样的语境。

(3) Procedures.

(3) 程序。

Procedures also improve communication. In particular, procedures are vital for communication without visual feedback.

程序也能改善沟通。特别是在没有视觉反馈的交流中，程序至关重要。

(4) Checklists.

(4) 执行检查单。

5.5 Conflict and Conflict Management
5.5 冲突和冲突管理

5.5.1 Definition
5.5.1 冲突的定义

Conflicts arise from the perception of incompatible needs or goals, and from the impossibility or failure to render them compatible. This applies to any difference in opinion about the mission and the crew's work, both inside and outside the cockpit. A conflict is not necessarily negative. It can even be helpful by bringing forward new points of view. Its negative effects result from poor management of antagonism.

冲突产生于对需求或目标的不一致的理解，也来自这些需求或目标调和的失败。在驾驶舱内，冲突是指机组成员之间意见的不一致，也包括相互不满或是较为过激的行为。飞行中的冲突对飞行安全的影响既有积极的也有消极的。显然，飞行中的冲突是不可避免地，冲突的负面影响主要是对冲突处理不当导致的。

5.5.2 Conflict Types
5.5.2 冲突的分类

Four conflict types are distinguished:

冲突有4种:

(1) Intra-personal: incompatible goals exist in one's head, e. g. , the desire to apply to a larger airline versus the risk of being fired if this attempt is known by the management.

(1) 个人内心的冲突：它指存在于个人头脑中矛盾的目标。如：想跳槽到大公司的愿望，一旦这种愿望被管理层知道就有可能面临被开除的危险之间的冲突。

(2) Inter-personal: two or more people perceive incompatible needs or goals and perceive potential interference from the tother in achieving their goals.

(2) 人与人之间的冲突：大家有不一致的需求和目标，并且在达到目标的过程中存在着来自他人的干扰。

(3) Intra-group: two or more people within a group perceive incompatible needs or goals.

(3) 团体内部的冲突：一个团体中的成员之间有不一致的需求和目标。

(4) Inter-group: conflicting goals are defined at the group level, e. g. , mergers.

(4) 团体之间的冲突：定位在团体层面的冲突，如合并。

5.5.3 Conflict Management Strategies and Skills
5.5.3 冲突管理策略和技巧

Conflict management skills are very important for safety. Several coping strategies are presented and defined hereafter. They may help to prevent the conflict from escalating and/or contribute to a smooth resolution:

冲突管理技能对飞行安全至关重要。以下应对策略有助于防止冲突升级和/或有助于顺利解决：

(1) Inquiry.

Inquiring is seeking information by questioning, interrogating, investigating, looking for facts, the reasons behind, in order to better understand each person's goals, motivations, needs and constraints.

(1) 质询。

质询是通过提问、询问、调查、寻找事实和背后的原因来寻求信息，以便更好地了解每个人的目标、动机、需求和限制。

(2) Advocacy.

Advocating consist of the protagonists pleading in favour of their own position, supporting and defending their point of view by argument.

(2) 辩论。

通过辩论来支持自己的立场，支持和捍卫自己的观点。

(3) Feedback.

Providing feedback is saying back to others what you have understand from them, and seeking corrective inputs.

(3) 反馈。

把你从交流对方了解到的信息再反馈给别人，以此寻求信息的正输入。

(4) Meta-communication.

Discuss a given object of communication itself or some aspect of it.

(4) 元信息传递。

讨论交流本身给定的目标。

(5) Negotiation.

Negotiation is the process by which two or more parties make attempts to define what each of them accepts to lose or to win in order to avoid a lose-lose outcome, or to leave the conflict unresolved.

(5) 协商。

协商是一个过程，通过两个或更多方试图阐述他们各自可以接受的后果，避免出现双输的结果，或让冲突无法得到解决。

(6) Compromise.

The best decision is the one that everyone naturally agrees upon.

(6) 仲裁。

最好的决策是大家达成共识。

Further Reading: Silent co-pilot in Airblue Flight 202
拓展阅读：蓝色航空 202 号航班上沉默的副驾驶

Airblue Flight 202 was a scheduled Airblue domestic passenger flight from Karachi's Jinnah International Airport to Islamabad's Benazir Bhutto International Airport. On 28 July 2010, the Airbus A321-231 narrow-body jet airliner serving the flight crashed near Islamabad, the capital of Pakistan, killing all 146 passengers and 6 crew on board. The aircraft crashed in the Margalla Hills north of Islamabad after air traffic controllers lost contact with the flight crew during their attempt to land in dense fog and heavy monsoon rain.

蓝色航空 202 号航班是从卡拉奇真纳国际机场飞往伊斯兰堡贝娜齐尔布托国际机场的国内定期航班。2010 年 7 月 28 日，空客 A321-231 窄体客机在巴基斯坦首都伊斯兰堡附近坠毁，机上 146 名乘客和 6 名机组人员全部遇难。飞机失联时，天气情况为浓雾和大雨，机组人员正在试图降落，最终这架飞机在伊斯兰堡北部的马加拉山坠毁。

The Pakistan Civil Aviation Authority (PCAA) issued the final report in November 2011. It covered the key events that led to the crash. The aircraft took off at 02:52 UTC. During the initial climb, the captain tested the knowledge of the first officer, and used harsh words in snobbish tones while speaking to him. This was very contrary to Airblue's procedures. The lecture continued for about one hour, with only brief intervals. After the humiliating session, the first officer remained mostly silent throughout the rest of the flight, likely from a loss of self esteem and confidence. Subsequently, the first officer did not challenge the captain over any of his errors or violations.

巴基斯坦民航局（PCAA）于 2011 年 11 月发布了最终报告，其中涵盖了导致坠机的关键事件。飞机于协调世界时 02：52 起飞。在最初的爬升过程中，机长测试了副驾驶的专业知识，副驾驶回答不理想，此后机长与副驾驶交谈时语气不好，使用了严厉的言语。这与蓝色航空的常规飞行程序截然相悖。训斥持续了大约一个小时，中间只有很短的停顿间隔。在被机长羞辱之后，副驾驶失去了自尊和信心，在接下来的飞行中几乎保持沉默。随后，副驾驶没有质疑机长的任何错误或违规行为。

While Flight 202 was descending to Islamabad, the captain decided to change the instrument landing approach to a visual circling approach. The captain checked the weather apprehensively, and asked the first officer to feed unauthorized waypoints in the FMS. The first officer did not challenge the captain for his incorrect actions (which may have been caused by the "lecturing session" earlier). The captain then briefed the first officer that he would turn the aircraft in the direction of Runway 30, later to abeam 5 nautical miles (9.3km) from the runway and then land.

当 202 航班下降到伊斯兰堡机场附近时，机长决定将仪表着陆方法更改为目视盘旋方法。机长担心地查看了天气，并要求副驾驶在 FMS 中输入未经授权的航路点。副驾驶没有质疑机长的错误行为（这可能是由之前的“被训”引起的）。然后机长告诉副驾驶，他将把飞机转向 30 号跑道的方向，然后在距跑道 5 海里（9.3 千米）处对正跑道，然后着陆。

However, this is contrary to the procedures in Islamabad for a visual approach. When a visual approach is executed, the plane automatically strings a final leg extending the runway centerline.

这种操作与伊斯兰堡机场的目视进近程序相反。执行目视进近时，飞机自动延长跑道中线串（造）出一条五边。

The captain then requested visual approach to Runway 12 (the request again being contrary to established procedures at Islamabad Airport), but this was not agreed to by the radardue to procedural limitations. The captain became worried about bad weather and low clouds on the left downwind approach. The aircraft then started its descent.

机长随后请求目视进近，使用 12 号跑道着陆（该请求再次违反伊斯兰堡机场的进近程序），由于程序限制，管制并未同意。机长开始担心左侧顺风进近时的恶劣天气和低云。飞机随后开始下降。

The captain wanted to descend to 2000ft (610m), but the first officer reminded him that the Minimum Descent Altitude (MDA) was 2500ft. However, later on, the plane descended through 2300ft (700m), thus violating the MDA of 2500ft (760m). After break-off from ILS approach, the captain ignored the tower controller's suggestion to fly a bad weather circuit by saying "let him say whatever he wants to say".

机长想下降到 2000 英尺（610 米），但副驾驶提醒他最低下降高度（MDA）为 2500 英尺。然而，机长还是操作飞机下降到 2300 英尺（700 米），违反了 2500 英尺（760 米）的 MDA 限制。在使用仪表着陆系统进近中断后终止仪表进近程序后，机长无视塔台管制员的建议，并说“让他说他想说的吧”。

The crew commanded a left turn to 300° through the autopilot. This could be done by rotating the heading knob of the aircraft to the heading that the crew wanted and subsequently pulling the knob, which would cause the plane to turn. However, because the crew forgot to pull the knob, the plane did not turn. A few seconds later, the first "terrain ahead" warning sounded. The first officer told the captain "Sir, higher ground has reached, sir, there is a terrain ahead, sir turn left". By now the captain had become very jittery in his verbal communication and displayed frustration, confusion and anxiety resulting in further deterioration in his behaviour.

机组人员通过自动驾驶左转 300°。这个操作可以通过将飞机的航向旋钮旋转到机组人员想要的航向后拉动旋钮来实现，这将导致飞机改变航向。然而，由于机组人员忘记拉旋钮，飞机没有转弯。几秒钟后，第一个“地形”警告响起。副驾驶告诉机长“机长，前面有山，机长，左转”。此时，机长的言语交流变得非常紧张，表现出沮丧、困惑和焦虑，导致他的操作行为能力进一步恶化。

Later on, the captain became confused due to several issues, including the tower repeatedly asking if the aircraft was in visual approach, the imminent collision with terrain, and the plane not turning on the heading it had been programmed to. The consequent loss of situational awareness caused the aircraft to go astray.

后来，机长对以下几个问题表示困惑，包括塔台反复询问飞机是否在目视进近，即将与地形发生碰撞，以及飞机没有按照输入的航向飞行。机长情景意识完全丧失，导致飞机误入歧途。

The aircraft ended up in a dangerous situation mostly because of unprofessional handling by the captain. Since the initiative of the first officer had been curbed and a communication barrier had already been created by the captain, the first officer failed to intervene and take over the controls to pull the aircraft out of danger and display the required Crew Resources Management (CRM) skills. During the last few seconds, the aircraft climbed to 3090 feet (940m) . The captain put in 52 degrees of bank to turn the aircraft, and also made some nose down inputs. Therefore, the aircraft pitched down, speed increased and auto thrust commanded the engines to spool down to keep airspeed on the target speed. The aircraft started to descend at a high rate. The aircraft then slammed into the Margala Hills and exploded.

这架飞机最终陷入绝境，主要是因为机长操作不专业。机长设置了沟通障碍，副驾驶的主动性被遏制，副驾驶未能干预并接管控制，也没有展现出可将飞机从危险中脱离所需的机组资源管理（CRM）技能。在最后几秒钟，飞机爬升到 3090 英尺（940m）。机长将飞机倾斜 52°以转动飞机，并且还进行了一些机头向下输入。因此，飞机俯仰，速度增加，自动推力命令发动机减速以保持空速在目标速度上。飞机开始高速下降。飞机随后撞上马加拉山并爆炸。

Flight Training Files
飞行训练档案

Case 1
案例1

Xiao Ming did glide approach with the instructor today, because the senior fellow taught Xiao Ming how to operate, and he had also watched some relevant videos, so he was confident before he got on the plane while considering that he would be praised for this class. During the flight, the instructor pointed out that Xiao Ming did not follow the SOP. Xiao Ming does not think so, he insisted that he was right in flight, then he didn't modify his operation according to the requirements of the instructor. After landing, the instructor failed Xiao Ming's lesson.

小明今天与教员飞无动力返场，因为学校的学长教过小明怎么飞这节课，并且小明自己也找过一些相关视频看过，所以他上飞机前胸有成竹，认为自己这节课一定会被表扬。而在飞行中教员指出小明没有按照航校 SOP 操作。小明不以为然，认为自己飞的是对的，依旧我行我素不按教员要求修改。落地后教员把小明这节课“挂”了。

Briefing
讲评

No matter what course it is, cadets should read SOP carefully beforehand. SOPs would be different between the flying schools. Senior fellows are not qualified instructors. There might be some differences between what the fellow was taught and what Xiao Ming was told. Even if he thought the instructor was wrong, he could talk with him, trying to give his own opinions.

无论什么课程，学员飞行前都应仔细按照航校 SOP 进行预习。由于航校不同，SOP 之间也会有些许区别。学校学长并无教员资质，小明所学的内容可能也与学长教的有一些出入。即使认为教员说法不对，也可以尝试与教员委婉沟通、探讨。

Case 2
案例2

Xiao Ming did a solo flight today, and joined downwind according to the instructions given by the tower. He heard the tower called his callsign when he was just about to turn base, followed by a long sentence. Xiao Ming didn't understand. He considered that the tower was telling him about the weather which didn't matter. Xiao Ming was embarrassed to let the tower say again, so read back his call sign then continued approaching. The tower called for another plane to go around after he had joined the base. Xiao Ming got the idea immediately that the controller let him extend his downwind to avoid collision with another high-performance aircraft which was on a direct approach. When landed, Xiao Ming was grounded by the flight school for a period of time.

小明今天还是飞单飞，返场时根据塔台指示加入了三边。快转四边时小明听到塔台报了他的呼号，叽里咕噜说了一堆。小明没听懂，他以为塔台在跟他报无关紧要的天气。小明不好意思让塔台复诵，所以回了个呼号就继续进近了。在他转到四边后塔台叫了另一架飞机让其复飞。小明这才反应过来，刚刚塔台让他延长三边避让五边直接进近的另一架高性能飞机。落地后小明被航校停飞了一段时间。

Briefing
讲评

Communication between pilots and air traffic controllers is vital. You can ask them to say again when you don't fully understand them. To ensure the flight safety, ten times' say again is also OK. You shouldn't ignore the instructions because of the face-saving issues or you simply think that's useless. For those clearances given by the controllers, pilots must fully readback, not responding the callsign only. During visual phrases, you should look out every time before you entering a turn, making sure there is no collision.

飞行员与管制之间的沟通是非常重要的。在未充分理解塔台指令时应该及时提出让对方复诵。为保证飞行安全，哪怕需要多次复诵也应该提出，不能因为碍于面子或主观认为是无用信息便主动过滤。对于管制给出的许可等指令，飞行员应全部复诵，不能只报呼号。在目视飞行过程中，每次转弯前都需要左顾右看，确保两边没有冲突。

Unit 3
Situational Awareness

第3篇　情景意识

Lead-in
课程导入

On August 27, 2006, about 06: 35 eastern daylight time, Comair flight 5191, a Bombardier CL-600-2B19, 2 N431CA, crashed during takeoff from Blue Grass Airport (LEX), Lexington, Kentucky. The flight crew was instructed to take off from runway 22 but instead lined up the airplane on runway 26 and began the takeoff roll. The airplane ran off the end of the runway and impacted the airport perimeter fence, trees, and terrain. The captain, flight attendant, and 47 passengers were killed, 3 and the first officer received serious injuries. The airplane was destroyed by impact forces and post-crash fire. Comair Flight 5191 was the third of a dozen early morning takeoffs scheduled at Lexington. The two previous planes used the longer runway without incident, the aviation source said.

2006年8月27日，大约东部夏令时06：35，Comair 5191号航班，庞巴迪CL-600-2B19，2 N431CA，在从肯塔基州列克星敦蓝草机场（LEX）起飞时坠毁。机组人员得到指令是从22号跑道起飞，但是他们却使用了26号跑道开始起飞滑跑。飞机冲出了跑道的尽头，撞到了机场周边的围栏、树木。机长、乘务员和47名乘客死亡，副驾驶和三名乘客受重伤。飞机被冲击力和坠机后的大火摧毁。Comair 5191号航班是当天清晨计划在列克星敦起飞的12架航班中的第三架。据称，前两架飞机都使用了较长的22号跑道，没有发生飞行事故。

The airport's two runways—one 3500 feet (1km) long, the other 7000 feet (2.1km) —intersect, and the pilots had been cleared to use the longer of the two.

该机场的两条跑道——一条3500英尺（1千米）长，另一条7000英尺（2.1千米）长——是两条交叉跑道，涉事飞行员被获准使用两条跑道中较长的一条进行起飞。

Runway 22, the air carrier runway, was 7000 feet long and 150 feet wide. It had high intensity runway lights. Runway 4/22 also had centerline lights and runway end identifier lights, but they were out of service at the time of the accident because of a construction project.

22号跑道是运输航空跑道，长7000英尺，宽150英尺。它有高强度道面灯，也有跑道4/22中心线灯和跑道头标识灯，但在事故发生时，由于施工，灯光系统已停止使用。

Runway 26, the general aviation runway, was used for about 2 percent of the airport's total operations. Runway 26 was 3500 feet long and 150 feet wide. Runway 26 was used only for flights conducted when daytime visual flight rules (VFR) prevailed, and for aircraft that weighed less than 12500 pounds. Although the runway was equipped with runway edge lights when the width was 150 feet, these lights had been disconnected since 2001 when the runway was designated for daytime VFR use only, as shown in Figure 1.

26号跑道为通用航空跑道，使用率约为机场总运营的2%。跑道长3500英尺，宽150英尺。26号跑道仅用于日间飞行，使用目视飞行规则（VFR），以及重量低于12500磅的飞机。由于26号跑道被指定为日间使用，因此从2001年起该跑道边线灯已关闭，如图1所示。

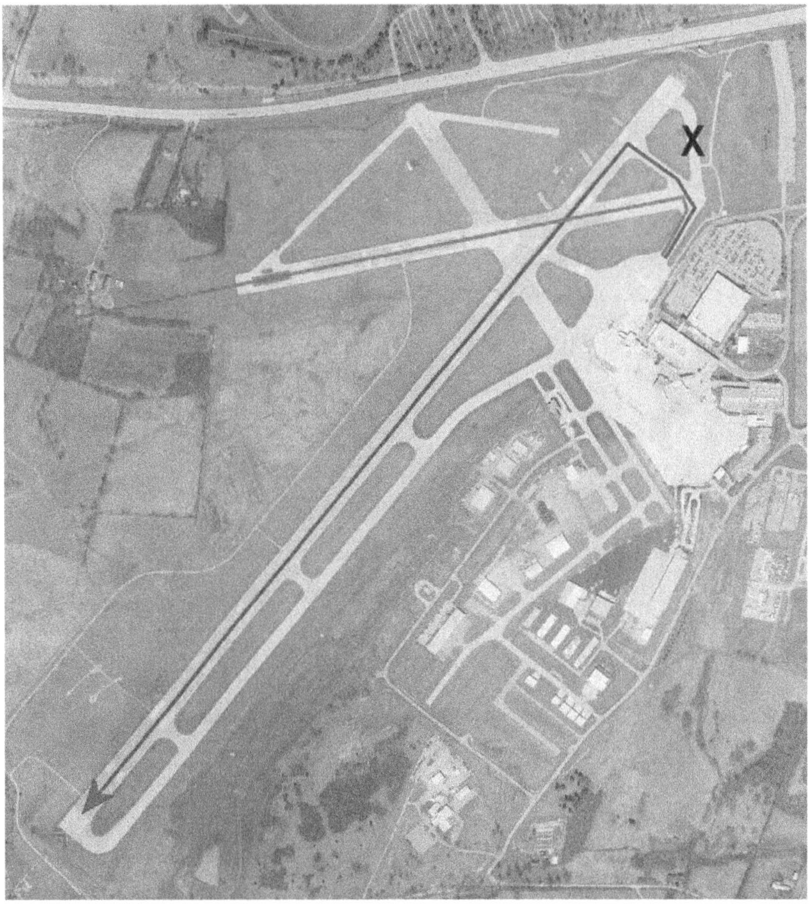

Figure 1 Two runway in Blue Grass Airport (LEX)
图1 Blue Grass 机场（LEX）的两条跑道

扫一扫查看彩图

During a public meeting on July 26, 2007, the NTSB announced the probable cause of the accident, as follows: The National Transportation Safety Board determines that the probable cause of this accident was the flight crewmembers'failure to use available cues and aids to identify the airplane's location on the airport surface during taxi and their failure to cross-check and verify that the airplane was on the correct runway before takeoff. Contributing to the accident were the flight crew's non-pertinent conversations during taxi, which resulted in a loss of positional awareness and the Federal Aviation Administration's failure to require that all runway crossings be authorized only by specific air traffic control clearances.

2007年7月26日，美国国家运输安全委员会在公开会议上公布了事故原因如下：美国国家运输安全委员会决定，这次事故的可能原因是飞行机组人员未能在滑行阶段使用可用的线索和帮助以确定飞机的位置，以及未能在起飞前再次确认和验证跑道是否正确。另外，机组人员在滑行过程中进行与飞行不相关的谈话，也是导致他们失去了位置意识的诱因。此外，美国联邦航空管理局并未要求飞机在跑道穿越过程中必须获得特定的管制许可。

Now, " confirm the runway number before entering the runway" and " confirm that the runway heading is consistent with the heading selected by the cockpit after aligning the runway" have become part of many airlines'standard procedures. During the ground taxiing phase of the accident, both the captain and the co-pilot are ignoring the cockpit regulations in the crucial flight stage and chatting freely - making them temporarily lose the ability to detect threats and potential risk. It often appears in: When flying in groups with acquaintances. When performing frequent flights. The most effective way is to follow standard CALL OUT , standard procedures and regulations. Therefore, adding relevant contents to the training can also play a good effect.

现在，“进入跑道前确认跑道号”和“对齐跑道后确认跑道方向与驾驶舱选择的航向一致”已经成为许多航空公司标准程序的一部分。在上述事故的地面滑行阶段，机长和副驾驶无视飞行的关键阶段应遵守的驾驶舱静默规则，随意聊天，使他们暂时失去了发现威胁和潜在风险的能力，这就带来了飞行的安全隐患。这种情况经常出现在与熟人一起飞行、飞行班次频繁的情形下。最有效的方法是遵循标准喊话、标准程序和规定。因此，在培训中增加相关内容也能起到很好的效果。

Key words

关键词

centerline lights	跑道中线灯
general aviation	通用航空
awareness	警觉、意识
runway heading	跑道方向
standard procedure	标准程序
standard CALL OUT	标准喊话

Discussion

讨论

(1) Accoring to what have discussed previously, what is the problem with crew communication?

(1) 根据我们前面学过的知识，本案例中飞行员的沟通和交流出现了什么问题?

(2) What is so called position awareness? Why do you think it is important in flight?

(2) 什么是所谓的位置意识? 它为什么会对飞行安全产生如此重要的影响?

(3) What kind of awareness should be held by pilots except position awareness?

(3) 除了位置意识，飞行员还应具备哪些意识?

(4) How to keep the good awareness in flight?

(4) 飞行中如何保持好的意识?

Advanced thinking

高阶思维

What can you learn from Figure 2?

What is the past, present, future situation information which should be taken into the Comair flight 5191 crew's consideration when they began to roll?

图2讲了什么?

作为Comair flight 5191的飞行员，在他们起飞滑跑的时候，他们应该获知哪些过去、现在、未来的情景?

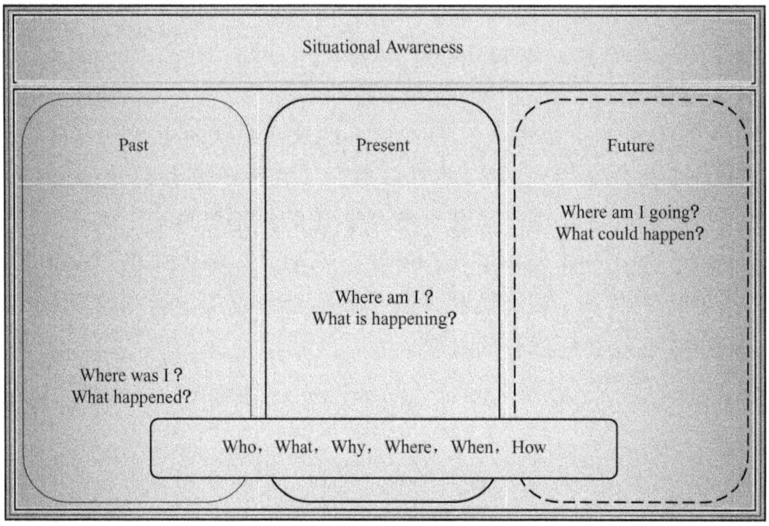

Figure 2 Situation awareness

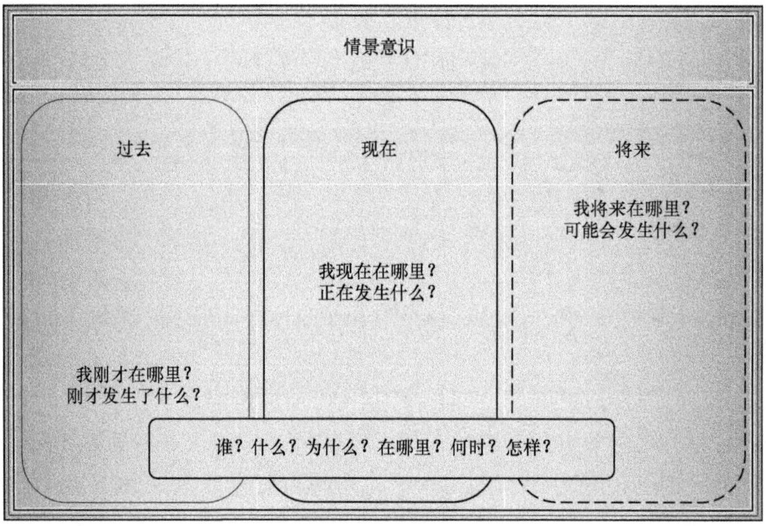

图2 情景意识

扫一扫查看彩图

Lesson 6 Basic Concepts
第 6 课 基本概念

6.1 Definition of Situational Awareness
6.1 情景意识的含义

Situational awareness is the accurate perception and understanding of all the factors and conditions within the five fundamental risk elements (flight, pilot, aircraft, environment, and type of operation that comprise any given aviation situation) that affect safety before, during, and after the flight. Monitoring radio communications for traffic, weather discussion, and ATC communication can enhance situational awareness by helping the pilot develop a mental picture of what is happening. It is a continuous perception of self and aircraft in relation to the dynamic environment of flight, threats (risks) and mission; and the ability to forecast and then execute tasks based on that perception.

情景意识是指飞行机组在特定的时段和特定的情境中对影响飞机和机组的各种因素、各种条件的准确知觉。通过收听航路上的通信、天气、空中交通管制信息，可以帮助飞行员在脑海中形成一个关于正在发生的事情的画面，从而提高情景意识。情景意识是一种居于飞行、威胁（风险）和任务等动态环境，关于飞行员自身和飞机状态的持续感知；以及能够基于这种感知进行预测并执行任务的能力。

Situational awareness is the accurate perception and understanding of all the factors and conditions within the four fundamental risk elements that affect safety before, during, and after the flight. To maintain situational awareness, a pilot needs to understand the relative significance of these factors and their future impact on the flight. When a pilot is situationally aware, he or she has an overview of the total operation.

既然情景感知是指在飞行前、飞行中和飞行后对影响安全的四个基本风险要素中的所有因素和条件的准确感知和理解，飞行员需要了解这些因素的相对重要性以及它们对飞行的未来影响才能保持情景意识感知。当飞行员有了情景下的感知时，他或她就会对飞行的整套操作有一个全面认知。

6.2 Categories of Situational Awareness
6.2 情景意识的分类

Please discuss the following statements。
请讨论以下几种说法是否正确。

(1) If the captain has a good situational awareness, the whole crew will have a good situational awareness.

(2) I am an observer and my situational awareness is not important.

(3) If the captain's situational awareness is not good, the whole flight won't go well.

(1) 机长的情景意识好，整个机组的情景意识就会好。

(2) 我是观察员，我的情景意识并不重要。

(3) 机长的情景意识不好，整个航班肯定会飞不好。

To discuss these issues, we first need to understand the classification of situational awareness. Situational awareness can be divided into individual situational awareness and group situational awareness, which are closely related and have certain differences.

要想讨论这几个问题，我们首先要了解情景意识的分类。情景意识有个体情景意识和群体情景意识之分，它们之间有密切的联系，也有一定的区别。

Individual Situational Awareness

A pilot's accurate perception and understanding of all the factors and conditions within the four fundamental risk elements that affect safety.

个体情景意识

某个飞行员对影响飞行环境的各种因素和各种条件的知觉。

Group Situational Awareness

It is the situational awareness of the crew as a whole.

群体情景意识

机组作为一个整体的机组所具有的情景意识。

For a two-man crew, the situational awareness of the two pilots may be different due to the different knowledge and experience, flight attitude and flight motivation of each pilot. In addition, situational awareness of pilots is not a fixed awareness, it is in constant change given by the factors of physiological, psychological, social and environmental issues.

对于双人制机组而言，由于每一个飞行员的知识经验、飞行态度、飞行动机不同，两位飞行员的情景意识可能有所差异。此外，飞行员的情景意识并不是固定不变的，它处于不断变化之中，引起这些变化的因素有生理性的，有心理性的，也有来自社会和环境方面的。

Flight safety depends on the situational awareness of the crew group, and further, the situational awareness level that the captain can obtain. This group situational awareness is not simply a superposition of each pilot's situational awareness.

飞行安全主要取决于机组群体情景意识，进一步而言，是机长所能获得的情景意识水平。这种群体情景意识不是简单地将每一个飞行员的情景意识叠加。

There are many factors that can affect a pilot's level of situational awareness, which we'll discuss in detail.

有许多因素会影响飞行员的情景意识水平，我们具体来讨论一下。

6.3 Factors Affecting Pilots' Situational Awareness
6.3 影响飞行员情景意识的因素

There are many factors that can affect a pilot's situational awareness, including the following five:

(1) Flight skills.

(2) Flight experience and training level.

(3) Spatial orientation ability.

(4) Health and attitude.

(5) Crew resource management.

有许多因素都会影响飞行员的情景意识水平，其中包括以下五点：

(1) 基本驾驶技术。

(2) 飞行经验和训练水平。

(3) 空间定向能力。

(4) 健康与态度。

(5) 机组资源管理。

Lesson 7 How to Deal with Loss of Situational Awareness
第7课 如何解决情景意识的丧失

7.1 Loss of Situational Awareness
7.1 情景意识的丧失

When you are flying, you can check out whether you have lost your situational awareness by asking yourself the questions as follows:

- Where are we now?
- Where are we going?
- What is the endurance of the aircraft?
- What's the weather like at the destination airport?
- How about obstacles?
- Can I trust what I see?
- What is the mode of automatic flight system now? What will be the next?
- What do I want to do with autopilot? Can I trust it?
- Who is flying the plane?
- Is that my job?
- Can I trust my partner?

在飞行中，你可以通过问自己以下这些问题来确认自己是不是丧失了情景意识。

- 我们现在在什么位置?
- 我们将要去哪里?
- 飞机的续航能力怎样?
- 目的地机场的天气怎样?
- 障碍物是什么情况?
- 我所看到的东西可信吗?
- 现在的自动飞行系统是什么方式? 下一种方式将会是什么?
- 我想要自动驾驶做什么? 我能否信任它?
- 谁正在操纵飞机?
- 那是我的分工吗?
- 我能信任搭档吗?

One of the greatest risks a pilot has when faced with a problem is that the pilot is simply not aware a problem exists. This undesired state is referred to as loss of situational awareness. Loss of situational awareness is like the boogieman sneaking up behind you——danger is imminent, but you are pleasantly unaware of it. Why does the pilot lose situational awareness?

在飞行中遇到问题时，飞行员面临的最大风险之一就是根本不知道飞行出现问题了。这种不被期待的飞行状态被称为情境意识的丧失。情景意识的丧失在你身后悄悄逼近——危险迫在眉睫，但你却没有意识到。哪些原因导致飞行员丧失情景意识呢？

Loss of situational awareness can be caused by something as simple as inattention. A pilot is not aware of the 12 o'clock, 1-mile target on a mid-air collision course because he or she hasn't been attentive in maintaining a traffic watch. A pilot not supervising the refuelling of the piston-engine aircraft is not aware that jet fuel has been loaded into the fuel tanks. A pilot inattentive during the pre-flight inspection is not aware that heavy rains and poor gas cap seals have conspired to put dangerous quantities of water in the fuel tanks.

情景意识的丧失可以由一些简单的事情引起，比如注意力不集中。因为飞行员没有注意收听无线电，飞行员就不知道一个在 12 点方向，距自己 1 英里处的目标可能与自己的飞机空中相撞。一名驾驶活塞式飞机的飞行员，如果没有监督飞机的加油，就不知道飞机燃油是否已经装进了油箱。一名飞行员在飞行前的检查中粗心大意，就无法意识到大雨和密封不良共同导致飞机油箱进水。

Loss of situational awareness is certainly a function of experience and training. A pilot on a fresh instrument rating is possibly unaware of just how rapidly dangerous amounts of ice can form on an aircraft after entering large cumulus clouds above the freezing level.

情景意识的丧失无疑是经验和训练不足的结果。一名刚刚获得仪表等级的飞行员可能不知道，当飞机在积冰层以上，会快速出现积冰现象。

An even more interesting cause of loss of situational awareness is false assumptions.

造成情境意识丧失的另一个原因是错误的假设。

Eastern Air Lines Flight 401 departed New York for Miami on December 29, 1972. The Lockheed L-1011 crashed into the Florida Everglades. Both pilots and the flight engineer died, along with 2 out of 10 flight attendants and 96 of the 163 passengers on board. There were 75 survivors. While the crew dealt with an inoperative landing gear indicator light, the plane's autopilot was accidentally disconnected. Flight crew didn't realize the plane was descending ("We're still at 2000, right?"). The crew of Eastern 401 thought the autopilot was still controlling the aircraft's altitude.

1972 年 12 月 29 日，美国东方航空公司的 401 航班从纽约飞往迈阿密。执飞的洛克希德公司出产的 L-1011 客机坠入佛罗里达大沼泽地。飞行员和飞行工程师都遇难了，机上 10 名空乘人员中有 2 人遇难，机上 163 名乘客中有 96 人遇难。事故有 75 名幸存者。事故原因是当机组人员处理一个失效的起落架指示灯时，飞机的自动驾驶仪不小心断开了。机组人员没有意识到飞机正在下降（“我们还在 2000 英尺，对吧?”）。美国东方航空 401 号航班的飞行员还以为飞机的自动驾驶正在控制着飞机的高度。

If the plane is still under the pilot's control but gets into an accident, it means the crew lost situational awareness. In addition, a number of accidents are caused by pilots losing control of aircraft. In many cases, loss of control of the aircraft is actually caused by loss of situational awareness. For example, not noticing the speed of the aircraft, the icing conditions, or the state or aircraft system or terrain.

如果飞机仍然是可以控制的却造成事故，这也就意味着机组失去了情景意识。另外，也有一部分事故是由于飞行员失去了对飞机的控制而造成的。在很多情况下，失去对飞机的控制事实上也是由于失去了情景意识造成的。例如：没有注意到飞机的速度、结冰情况、飞机系统或者地形。

Here are some of the factors that are commonly at the root of false assumptions:

以下是一些常见的导致错误假设的因素：

(1) Uncontrolled aircraft or unmonitored cockpit: During flight, if the crew members are not operating the aircraft or monitoring the cockpit environment, the crew may lose some important information, resulting in a loss of situational awareness.

(1) 无人操纵飞机或者无人监视驾驶舱：在飞行中，如果机组成员当没有人操作飞机或者是监视驾驶舱的环境就可能使机组丧失对某些重要的信息的觉察，从而导致情景意识下降。

(2) Impulsive behavior or confusion: Impulsive behavior is a lack of conscious control of the behavior, which also indicates that our situational awareness may be lost.

(2) 冲动性行为或者是混淆：冲动性行为是一些缺少意识控制的行为，这些行为也正表明我们的情景意识可能丧失了。

(3) Fixation or concentration: A condition where we are so focused on a task that we may miss important information.

(3) 固执或者是全神贯注：是一种将所有精力集中于某个任务的表现，这种状况可能让我们忽略某些重要的信息。

(4) When the reliable system fails.

(4) 可靠系统出现故障时。

(5) Inconsistent with established goals, unexpected results at unusual times.

(5) 与既定目标不吻合，在不正常的时机有不期望的结果出现。

(6) Ambiguous or semantically ambiguous information.

(6) 模棱两可的信息或是语义模糊。

When you lose situational awareness, don't try to figure out the consequences. You have better things to do because of time limitation.

Maintains a stable, safe and simple situation is the primary task.

Recognizes your limitations, speak out your doubts and listens to others.

If both crew members have poor situational awareness at the same time, approach the ATC, the operating department or another aircraft in the air to avoid dwelling on a past problem. You still have sufficient time to comment on what has happened after flight.

当你失去情景意识时，你不要试图去想后果如何。时间不允许，你还有更重要的事去做。

保持情况的稳定、安全和简单化是首要任务。

认识到你的局限性，讲出你的疑惑并且聆听他人意见。

如果两个机组成员的情景意识同时都比较差，可以向 ATC、运行部门或空中的其他飞机求助，避免一直纠缠于已经发生的问题。待飞行任务结束后，你会有足够的时间讲评这次飞行。

7.2　Approaches to Improve Situational Awareness
7.2　提高飞行机组情景意识的方法

Solid knowledge of aviation theory is an important prerequisite for establishing situational awareness. As the flight system and flight environment become more and more complex, these changes put forward new requirements for the knowledge accomplishment of pilots. Only with solid knowledge of aviation theory, pilots can make reasonable explanations for various phenomena and establish a good situational awareness.

扎实的航空理论知识是建立情景意识的重要前提。由于飞行系统和飞行环境越来越复杂，这些变化对飞行员的知识素养提出了新的要求，只有具备扎实的航空理论知识，飞行员才能够对发生的各种现象做出合理的解释，建立良好的情景意识。

Establishing situational awareness through initial flight training. Flight training is not only a way for pilots to acquire flight skills, but also an important way for pilots to acquire situational awareness. Pilots should cultivate their situational awareness consciously at all stages of flight training.

通过初始飞行训练建立良好的情景意识。飞行训练是飞行员获得操纵技术的途径，同时也是飞行员获得情景意识的重要途径。在飞行训练的所有阶段飞行员都应该有意识地培养自己的情景意识。

Through the proper use of cockpit resource management tools: cockpit communication, inquiry and response, short-term strategy.

通过合理使用驾驶舱资源管理的工具：驾驶舱交流、质询与反应、短期策略。

7.3　Maintaining Situational Awareness
7.3　如何保持情景意识

Fatigue, stress, and work overload can cause a pilot to fixate on a single perceived important item and reduce an overall situational awareness of the flight. A contributing factor in many accidents is a distraction that diverts the pilot's attention from monitoring the instruments or scanning outside the aircraft. Many flight deck distractions begin as a minor problem, such as a gauge that is not reading correctly, but result in accidents as the pilot diverts attention to the perceived problem and neglects to properly control the aircraft.

疲劳、压力和超负荷工作可能会导致飞行员专注飞行中的某一重要项目，从而降低对飞行的整体情景的感知。飞行事故的原因之一就是飞行员的注意力分散，即注意力从监测仪表或扫视飞机外形任务中移开。在驾驶舱中许多干扰一开始只是一个小问题，比如仪表读数不正确，但由于飞行员将注意力转移到感知飞行中出现的问题上，从而忽视了对飞机的控制，就会导致飞行事故。

There are some tips for maintaining situational awareness.

(1) Distraction management.

(2) Stress management.

(3) Good communication.

(4) Workload management.

(5) Good judgment and decision making.

(6) Problem solving ability.

(7) Good flight planning and monitoring.

(8) Effective crew resource management.

下面是一些保持情景意识的方法。

(1) 管理好注意力分散。

(2) 应激管理。

(3) 良好的交流。

(4) 工作负荷的管理。

(5) 良好的判断与决策。

(6) 问题解决。

(7) 做好飞行计划和进程监控。

(8) 有效的机组资源管理。

Lesson 8　Pilot Distractions
第 8 课　注意力分散

8.1　Unsafe Situations Resulting From Pilot Distractions
8.1　注意力分散引发的后果

The following are examples of unsafe situations resulting from pilot distractions:

- Runway incursion.
- Incorrect aircraft configuration for takeoff.
- Late landing gear retraction.
- Premature or delayed slats/flaps retraction.
- Flaps placard-speed (VFE) exceedance.
- Late response to ATC instructions.
- Failure to select engine anti-ice when required.
- Altitude/flight level "bust" in climb or descent.
- Inadequate fuel management (e. g. , late detection of fuel imbalance).
- Speed below minimum during descent.
- Failure to reset altimeter.
- Altitude deviation or stall during holding pattern.
- Late aircraft configuration for landing.
- Failure to capture glide slope.
- Descent below MDA.
- Taxiway excursion.
- Failure to set parking brake on arrival at gate or parking stand.

以下是由于注意力分散而造成的不安全事件:

- 跑道入侵。
- 飞机起飞构型不正确。
- 起落架收起晚。
- 缝翼/襟翼过早或延迟收回。
- 襟翼超速。
- 对空管指令响应偏晚。
- 没有及时使用发动机防冰。
- 爬升或下降时不能保持高度/高度层。
- 燃油管理不当(没有及时监控到燃油不平衡)。
- 下降时飞机速度低于最小速度。

- 没有及时调置高度表拨正值。
- 高度偏离或在等待航线中出现失速。
- 着陆时飞机组态偏晚。
- 未能捕获下滑坡道。
- 高度下降低于 MDA。
- 滑错滑行道。
- 到达停机坪后没有设置停留刹车。

8.2 General Strategies for Reducing Distractions
8.2 减少注意力分散的策略

There are no absolute methods to prevent or control pilot distractions. The effectiveness of efforts will depend to some extent on factors such as an airline's operating environment, prevailing rules and the cultural background of the crewmembers. Nevertheless, there are some good general rules to follow including:

我们没有绝对的方法来防止或控制飞行员注意力分散。方法是否有效在一定程度上取决于航空公司的运营环境、通行规则和机组人员的文化背景等因素。尽管如此，有一些一般规则需要我们去遵循，包括：

Adhere to the Sterile Cockpit Rule (U. S. FAR - Part 121.542) as an integral part of SOPs because it has the potential to reduce interruptions and distractions. The Sterile Cockpit Rule limits unnecessary conversations and communications during taxi, takeoff, landing and below 10000 feet.

作为标准操作规程的一个组成部分，驾驶舱静默原则可以降低注意力分散。它限制了在滑行、起飞、着陆的所有地面操作阶段以及 10000 英尺以下的所有不能进行不必要的交谈的操作阶段。

Avoid the most frequent causes of pilot distractions including:

请避免以下引发飞行员注意力分散的因素：

Non-flight-related conversations.

与飞行无关的谈话。

Distractions by cabin crewmembers.

乘务组的打扰。

Non-flight-related radio calls.

与飞行无关的通信。

Non-essential public-address (PA) announcements.

与飞行不相关的客舱广播。

There are specific ways to help control each of the major factors that promote interruptions and distractions discussed earlier.

针对这四个因素，给出一些防范策略。

（1） Communications.

（1） 交流。

Brief all jump-seat riders on the Sterile Cockpit Rule.

Put headsets on during critical phases of flight (e. g. , for any operations below 10000ft).

Plan PA announcements for low workload periods.

Keep intra-cockpit communications brief, clear and concise.

Pause or end conversations in advance of approaching the next defined target or the next altitude.

与观察员简要说明遵守驾驶舱静默原则。

飞行关键阶段佩戴耳机（10000英尺以下的任何操作阶段）。

在工作负荷较低的时候进行客舱广播。

驾驶舱交流内容简明清晰。

当接近下一个目标点或下一个高度时暂停或中断交流。

（2） Head-down activity.

（2） 埋头工作。

Define an SOP for task sharing when programming or reprogramming the FMS depending on the level of automation being used and the flight phase.

Plan extended head-down tasks for low workload periods.

Announce when you are going "head down".

根据自动化程度以及所处飞行阶段，明确FMS输入或者再次输入的任务分工。

在低工作负荷时低头操作。

告知机组你在低头操作。

（3） Responding to an abnormal condition or to an unanticipated situation.

（3） 对非正常或未预见的情况做出反应。

Keep the autopilot engaged to decrease workload unless otherwise required.

Adhere to PF/PNF task sharing for abnormal/emergency conditions (e. g. , PNF should maintain situational awareness, monitor and back up the PF).

Pay particular attention to the proper completion of normal checklists.

Handling an abnormal condition has a tendency to disrupt the normal flow of actions as specified in SOPs.

除出现特殊情况，要保持自动驾驶，降低工作负荷。

遵循非正常或紧急情况下的操纵飞行员（PF）/与监控飞行员（PNF）的任务分工（比如，PNF应保持情景意识，对PF进行监督和提醒）。

特别要注意正常检查单。

在非正常情景下，操作飞机可能会影响到标准操作程序中规定的正常流程。

（4） Search for Traffic.

（4） 寻找其他飞机。

Express a clear and loud "I fly, you watch" call when required to search for traffic by a

TCAS alert or a call from ATC.

当交通管制员通知有飞机或是空中防撞系统告警时，大声且清晰喊话："我操纵，你观察"。

8.3 Managing/Mitigating Pilot Distractions
8.3 管理/缓解飞行员注意力分散

Some interruptions and distractions are subtle and potentially difficult to detect. The first priority, therefore, must be to recognize that a disruption has, in fact, occurred. Once you are aware that the normal flow of activities has been interrupted, the second priority is to re-establish situational awareness.

有些干扰和注意力分散是微妙的，可能难以察觉。因此，首要任务必须是发现并识别干扰和注意力分散。一旦意识到正常的活动被打断了，第二项任务就是重新建立情景意识。

This is accomplished through the following steps:

(1) Identify—What was I doing?

(2) Ask—Where was I interrupted?

(3) Decide/Act—What decision or action shall I take to get "back on track?"

可以通过以下步骤实现：

(1) 识别——我在做什么？

(2) 提问——我在哪里被打断了？

(3) 决定/行动——我应该做什么决定或行动来"回到正轨"？

When deciding on an action:

(1) Use the clear guidelines in operations golden rules—"fly, navigate, communicate and manage systems, in that order".

(2) Plan all activities. Be willing to postpone some actions until time and conditions are more conducive.

(3) Ask for more time (e.g., from the ATC or from the other crewmember) to prevent being rushed.

(4) Follow SOPs to verify that any postponed action(s) have been accomplished.

当你决定要采取行动的时候：

(1) 使用明确的指导方针——"依据飞行、导航、沟通和管理系统的顺序进行"。

(2) 制订全局计划。愿意推迟一些行动，直到时间和条件都比较有利的时候再继续做。

(3) 申请更多的时间（例如，向空中交通管制员或其他机组人员），以避免仓促。

(4) 按照标准操作规程核实所有被推迟的操作是否已经完成。

8.4 Workload Management
8.4 工作负荷的管理

Effective workload management ensures essential operations are accomplished by planning, prioritizing, and sequencing tasks to avoid work overload. As experience is gained, a pilot learns to recognize future workload requirements and can prepare for high workload periods during times of low workload. Reviewing the appropriate chart and setting radio frequencies well in advance of when they are needed helps reduce workload as the flight nears the airport. In addition, a pilot should listen to ATIS, Automated Surface Observing System (ASOS), or Automated Weather Observing System (AWOS), if available, and then monitor the tower frequency or Common Traffic Advisory Frequency (CTAF) to get a good idea of what traffic conditions to expect. Checklists should be performed well in advance so there is time to focus on traffic and ATC instructions. These procedures are especially important prior to entering a highdensity traffic area, such as Class B airspace.

有效的工作负荷管理确保通过计划、优先级和排序任务来完成基本的操作，以避免超负荷工作。随着经验的积累，飞行员学会识别未来的工作量需求，并能在低工作量时就为高工作量的到来做好准备。提前查看合适的航图和设置无线电频率，有助于在航班接近机场时减少工作量。此外，飞行员应监听情报通播（ATIS）、自动地面观测系统（ASOS）或自动天气观测系统（AWOS），收听塔台频率或通用交通提示频率（CTAF），以更好地了解预计的交通状况。检查清单应该提前做好，这样就有时间关注飞机的动态和空中交通管制指令。在进入高密度交通区域（如B类空域）之前，这些程序尤其重要。

Recognizing a work overload situation is also an important component of managing workload. The first effect of high workload is that the pilot may be working harder but accomplishing less. As workload increases, attention cannot be devoted to several tasks at one time, and the pilot may begin to focus on one item. When a pilot becomes task saturated, there is no awareness of input from various sources, so decisions may be made on incomplete information and the possibility of error increases.

认识到工作负荷过大也是管理工作负荷的一个重要组成部分。工作量过大的第一个影响是，飞行员可能在飞行中投入精力更多，但完成的任务却更少。随着工作量的增加，注意力不能同时集中在几个任务上，飞行员可能会注意力分散到另一个任务上。当一个飞行员任务量饱和时，飞行员无法察觉到来自不同来源的所有信息输入，因此可能基于不完整的信息上做出决策，出现差错的可能性增加。

When a work overload situation exists, a pilot needs to stop, think, slow down, and prioritize. It is important to understand how to decrease workload. Placing a situation in the proper perspective, remaining calm, and thinking rationally are key elements in reducing stress and increasing the capacity to fly safely. This ability depends upon experience, discipline, and training.

当工作超负荷的情况存在时，飞行员需要停下来，思考，放慢速度，分清轻重缓急。飞行员了解如何减少工作量是很重要的一件事。从正确的角度看待情况，保持冷静，理性思考是减轻压力和提高安全飞行能力的关键因素。这种能力取决于飞行员自身的经验、规章意识和训练情况。

Flight Training Files
飞行训练档案

Case 1
案例1

Xiao Ming and the instructor are flying cross-country, the instructor praised Xiao Ming in the air. Xiao Ming was so proud that he found himself get lost after chatting with the instructor. Xiao Ming quickly lowered his head to search frantically on the map with heart pounding. "Where are we?" asked his instructor. Xiao Ming panicked and pointed at the map randomly, but he happened to be right, which frightened Xiao Ming badly.

小明与教员在飞一班转场，教员在空中夸赞小明经过学习后飞得不错。小明得意得不行，与教员闲聊几句后就发现自己迷航了。小明赶紧低头在地图上疯狂寻找，心怦怦直跳。恰逢此时教员问他："我们在哪?"小明慌了神在地图上胡乱一指，竟碰巧被他蒙对了，吓得小明出了一身冷汗。

Briefing
讲评

Cross-country means a long flight departing from the base airport, heading to others. Lost is a kind of situation which you can't tell where you are. That's usually due to the loss of situation awareness. Remaining the SA, then chat with the instructor. Don't panic when you face problems. Do something to fix it according the SOP and course requirements. Stay humble even you get praised, keep working hard to build up your skills.

转场意为去基地以外机场的长时间飞行。迷航就是找不到自己的位置。这大多是由于在飞行中的情景意识丧失。飞行中应始终保持情景意识，在保证飞行状态的情况下再和教员闲聊。如果遇到问题不要慌张，冷静地根据 SOP 和课程要求及时补救。在得到表扬时保持谦虚，继续努力夯实飞行技术。

Case2
案例 2

During a solo flight, the course minimum requires a Touch&Go at another airport. Xiao Ming expertly did the approach, deploying flaps, and made a perfect landing. He taxied and shut down, went to the toilet and started up again. But during the takeoff, he found his aircraft lift off uncontrollably. It turned out to be that he didn't retract the flaps up. He was taking off with full flaps. What should he do now?

一班单飞中，科目要求小明要在外场（训练基地以外的机场）做一个 Touch&Go。小明熟练地进近，放襟翼，做出一个完美的落地。小明滑出跑道、关车，上厕所回来开车、滑进跑道，所有动作一气呵成。然而当他在起飞过程中，却发现还没到抬轮速度的飞机自己飘了起来。原来是襟翼没有收起，小明在以满襟翼起飞。此时小明应该怎么办?

Briefing
讲评

Taking off with full flaps goes against the SOP accompanied with lots of risks. Cadets in solo phrases are easy to miss items in the checklist because they are unfamiliar with the checklists either tension. Given Cessna 172, usually, we only use 10 degrees flaps maximum for takeoff. Larger flap settings would decrease the rotate speed which might cause a stall. When in this situation, we should choose less than normal takeoff angles to avoid stall. Do not retract the flaps at once, or the sudden loss of lift would make the aircraft sink without of control. Also, it's important to learn how to correctly use the school checklists, following the SOP.

满襟翼起飞是违背 SOP 的做法，也是有很大风险的行为。在单飞阶段积攒经验的学员们由于对检查单的不熟练、又或是由于单飞的紧张，在单飞过程中很容易漏做、少做检查内容。一般来说即使用 C172 在短跑道起飞，我们只会选择 10°襟翼。过大的襟翼使抬轮速度变小，一不留神就会导致失速。遇到这种情况时，应该用较正常起飞时更小的角度爬升避免失速，并且不要将襟翼一下收完，否则瞬间失去的升力会使飞机不受控地下沉。最重要的还是熟悉并正确应用学校检查单，遵守 SOP 操作。

Case3
案例 3

Xiao Ming passed the private pilot exam, and began to do a solo flight. Xiao Ming had to get up early to fly every day. He had only one- or two-days' rest after a long-time flight in a week. After the flight, Xiao Ming went back to the dormitory to eat something in a rush and fell asleep. If you were Xiao Ming, what should you do?

小明通过了私照考试，开始了单飞阶段。飞五休二甚至飞六休一的日子让小明应接不暇，小明每天都需要起个大早去飞一班。飞完后午饭时间也过了，小明回到寝室随便吃点就困得睡着了。如果你是小明你该怎么办？

Briefing
讲评

It could be extremely hard based on school schedules. Alternate work with rest during the day-offs. If you feel unwell, report to your instructor or school, ask for a schedule change or a rest.

根据航校安排，在单飞期间可能会特别辛苦。在飞行间隔中，合理安排休息时间劳逸结合。如果出现身体不适的情况，及时与教员/航校反映，申请换班/休息。

Unit 4

Pilot Judgement and Aeronautical Decision Making

第4篇　判断与决策

Lead-in
课程导入

A ***private pilot*** with around 350 hours was flying an airplane ***cross-country***. Due to time constraints, the pilot skipped dinner the night before and had no breakfast on the morning of the flight. The pilot planned to have lunch around noon at a fuel stop.

一名有着 350 小时飞行经历的**私照阶段飞行员**正在执行一次**转场飞行**。由于准备时间不充裕，飞行员前一天晚上没有吃晚餐，当天早上也没有吃早餐。他计划到了中午找一个加油点再吃午饭。

A descent was begun from 9500 feet, about 20 miles from the chosen fuel stop, due to ***haze*** and unfamiliarity with the area. When the airplane arrived at ***pattern altitude***, the pilot could not find the airport. The pilot then circled north of the town, then back over the town, then flew to the west, then turned back to the east.

由于**雾霾**以及飞行员对该地区的不熟悉，飞机从 9500 英尺的高空开始下降，此时距离选定的加油点还有 20 英里。当飞行高度到达**起落航线高度**时，飞行员没有找到机场。他在小镇的北部开始盘旋，然后回到小镇上空，然后向西飞去，最后再返回到东部。

The pilot decided to check for airport information in the ***Airport/Facility Directory***, which was on the rear seat and not readily available. Power had not been increased since the descent to pattern altitude, and the pilot had been holding back pressure on the ***yoke***. While attempting to reach the Airport/Facility Directory, a loud "bang" was heard.

飞行员决定使用**机场细则**查找机场信息，而此时该目录被放在后座上，飞行员无法够到。自飞机降落到起落航线高度后，动力没有增加，飞行员一直拉着**操纵杆**。当他试图伸手抓那本机场/设施目录时，一声巨响突然响起。

Looking up, the pilot discovered the airplane was only about 200 feet above ground level. Increasing power, the pilot climbed and located the airport. After landing, it was discovered a fiberglass ***antenna*** had been hit, which damaged the ***leading edge*** of the left wing.

飞行员抬头一看，发现飞机离地面只有大约 200 英尺。飞行员加了油门，确定了机场的位置。飞机着陆后，他发现一个飞机上玻璃纤维**天线**被击中，损坏了左翼的**前缘**。

Key words
关键词

private pilot	私照阶段飞行员
cross-country	转场飞行
haze	霾
pattern altitude	起落航线高度
Airport/Facility Directory	机场细则
yoke	操纵杆
antenna	天线
leading edge	（机翼）前缘

Discussion
讨论

(1) Can you identify the judgement errors contributing to the final outcome of the flight?
(1) 你能否分辨飞行员的哪些判断错误影响了本次飞行?
(2) What is the relevant information a pilot should gather before flight?
(2) 在飞行前，飞行员应该收集哪些相关信息?
(3) What are the factors affecting pilots'decision in flight?
(3) 影响飞行员决策的因素有哪些?
(4) How to make a good decision in flight?
(4) 如何制定正确的飞行决策?

Advanced thinking
高阶思维

By discussing the events that led to thisincident, it can be understood how a series of judgmental errors contributed to the final outcome of this flight.

讨论本次事故征候，看看这一连串的判断错误是如何影响本次飞行的。

1.__________

The pilot understood it could affect the ability to fly safely, but let the desire to stay on schedule override the concern for a safe flight.

飞行员明知它的重要，却依旧将执行飞行计划凌驾于确保飞行安全之上。

2.__________

A quick review before descent, could have ensured a clear mental picture of the location of the airport in relation to the town.

在降落前快速回顾，可以确保脑海中有对机场相对于小镇具体位置的准确构图。

3.__________

It would have had the flight guide and any other necessary information near at hand.

应该将飞行手册和其他重要资料放在手边。

4.__________

Clearly that would include adjusting the power, setting the trim, and keeping track of altitude.

包括调整发动机功率、配平、保持高度。

Discuss the following questions with your partner.

与同伴讨论以下问题。

Are you a decision maker?

你是一个决策者吗?

Have you ever made a bad decision?

你做过失败的决策吗?

Do decision makers make mistakes?

决策者会犯错吗?

Tell us about a life-changing decision you have made for yourself.

告诉我们一个你自己制订的改变你生活命运的决策。

Who makes the decision on the flight deck?

驾驶舱里谁是决策者?

Do you prefer to take time over decisions you have made?

你在决策的时候会投入时间精力吗?

Describe the process you use to make the right decision?

请描述你做决策的整个过程。

How to make a right decision?

如何正确决策?

Lesson 9　Basic Concepts
第9课　基本概念

9.1　What is Judgement
9.1　什么是判断

A safe pilot consistently makes good judgments. What is good judgment? It is the ability to make an "instant" decision, which assures the safest possible continuation of the flight. But judgment may often be a series of evaluations, made over a period of minutes, hours, or even longer, that keeps you out of danger. Good judgment is an intangible component of flying which enhances safety. Good judgment can be the lifesaving edge in the midst of an unforeseen situation. While aviation flying is a safe mode of transportation, accident statistics indicate that the vast majority of accidents involve pilot error. Airmen who are either unaware of the potential hazards or who actually relish the opportunity to take unnecessary risks are those likely to be involved in judgment-error accidents. Through education and experience, pilots and pilots-to-be can learn good judgment just as thoroughly as they learn the mechanical concepts and basic skills of flying. In fact, learning judgment is just as much an important part of flying as learning to make good takeoffs and landing.

一个有着安全飞行意识的飞行员总是能做出正确的判断。什么是良好的判断力？这是一种做出“即时”决定的能力，能够确保飞行尽可能安全地继续下去。通常来说，判断是由一系列的评估构成的，飞行员要对未来几分钟、几小时甚至更长时间内会发生的事情做出能够远离危险的正确判断。良好的判断力是提高飞行安全性的组成部分。在无法预知的情形中，良好的判断力可以为挽救生命提供保障。航空飞行是一种安全的运输方式，但事故统计表明，绝大多数事故都与飞行员的失误有关。判断失误的飞行员往往没有意识到潜在危险，或是他们本来就享受冒险的飞行。对于飞行员或是飞行学员而言，良好的判断力和飞行知识及技能一样，都是可以通过学习的深入、飞行经历增加而掌握。事实上，拥有良好的判断力和掌握良好的起飞和降落技能一样，都是飞行的重要组成部分。

Judgment is not easily defined. One definition is that judgment is good, common "sense" as applied to the making of decisions, especially correct decisions. "Sense" relates to an intense awareness, realization, and understanding of all the factors which are involved in making a correct decision. In making a decision, pilots must consider all relevant intrapersonal, aircraft, and environmental factors which have, or may have, an influence upon his or her decision-making process. Pilot judgment is thus a process which produces a thoughtful, considered decision relating to the aircraft's operation along with an inseparable response (i. e., action/inaction) to that decision. Taking the viewpoint, then, that good pilot judgment is a process which involves thoughtful consideration and an outcome, a definition emerges:

我们很难说清楚到底什么是判断。有人认为，判断是那些用于制定良好决策的常识。这里的“意识”指的是对做出正确决策起到影响作用的所有因素产生的强烈意识、认识和理解。在做决定时，飞行员必须考虑所有已经或将会对他或她的决策过程产生影响的相关的个人、飞机和环境因素。这样看来，飞行员的判断是一个过程，它是一个经过深思熟虑后的决定，这个决定与飞机操作有关，并对该决定给出反应（即行动/不行动）。那么，好的飞行员判断是一个过程，包含了深思熟虑的考虑和结果，由此，判断的定义应为：

Pilot judgment is the process of recognizing and analyzing all available information about oneself, the aircraft, and the flying environment followed by the rational evaluation of alternatives to implement a timely decision which maximizes safety.

飞行员判断是识别和分析有关飞行员、飞机和飞行环境的所有可用信息，合理评估备选方案、及时实施确保飞行安全决策的过程。

Defining judgment is not a simple task. Difficulty arises when trying to distinguish among judgment, decision making, pilot judgment and aeronautical decision making. The terms are often used interchangeably.

判断并不是一项简单的任务。人们很难区分判断、决策、飞行员判断和决策，这些术语经常被交换使用。

Pilot judgment (Jensen 1995) — the mental process we use in making decisions:

Rational judgment — the ability to discover and establish the relevance of all available information relating to problems of flight, to diagnose these problems, to specify alternative courses of action and to assess the risk associated with each alternative.

Motivational judgment — the motivation to choose and execute a suitable course of action within the available time frame. The choice could be either action or no action, and "suitable" is a choice consistent with societal norms.

1995年，Jensen提出，飞行员判断力就是飞行员在做决定时的心理过程，这个过程中有理性判断和动机判断。

理性判断：判断飞行中的问题，指定行动方案以及评估与每个可选方案相关的分析的能力。

动机判断：在可用的时间内选择和执行一个合适的行动的动机。选择可以是行动或不行动，而“合适”是一种符合社会规范的选择。

Good pilot judgment requires the ability and motivation to:

(1) Discover and establish the relevance of all available information relating to problems of flight.

(2) Diagnose problems.

(3) Specify alternative courses of action.

(4) Assess the risk associated with each alternative.

(5) Choose and execute a suitable course of action within the available time (Jensen, 1995).

Jensen 提出，良好的飞行员判断力需要具备以下能力和动机：

（1）发现并确定与飞行问题有关的所有可用信息的相关性。

（2）诊断问题。

（3）明确可选择的行动方案。

（4）评估与每个备选方案相关的风险。

（5）在可用时间内选择并执行合适的行动方案。

9.2 What is Aeronautical Decision Making（ADM）
9.2 什么是决策

FAA Advisory Circular 60-22 on Aeronautical Decision Making（FAA Advisory Circular 60-22）states that ADM is a systematic approach to the mental process used by all involved in aviation to consistently determine the best course of action for a given set of circumstances.

美国联邦航空局关于航空决策的咨询通告 60-22 中指出，航空决策（ADM）是一种系统化的思维过程方法，所有航空相关人员都使用它来确定特定环境下的最佳行动方案。

What does that really mean? From the moment your feet hit the floor in the morning until the key is safely back in your pocket at the end of each flight, you as the pilot（or crew member）have a never-ending series of decisions to make. The process of good ADM is a continuous flow of information in and actions out.

这意味着什么呢？从你起床的那一刻，直到每次飞行结束时，作为飞行员（或机组成员）的你总是要不停地做一系列的决定。良好的航空决策是信息不断输入和行动的不断输出。

9.3 Hazard and Risk
9.3 危险与风险

9.3.1 What is Hazard
9.3.1 什么是危险

Two defining elements of ADM are hazard and risk. Hazard is a real or perceived condition, event, or circumstance that a pilot encounters. When faced with a hazard, the pilot makes an assessment of that hazard based upon various factors.

ADM 涉及了两个要素，分别是危险和风险。危险是飞行员遇到的真实的或可感知的情况或事件。当面临危险时，飞行员根据各种因素对危险进行评估。

Therefore, risk is an assessment of the single or cumulative hazard facing a pilot。

因此，风险是飞行员对面临的单一或多个危险给出的评估。

For example, the pilot arrives to preflight and discovers a small, blunt type nick in the leading edge at the middle of the aircraft's propeller. The nick is the hazard（a present condition）. The risk is propeller fracture if the engine is operated with damage to a propeller blade.

例如，飞行员在起飞前发现飞机螺旋桨中间的前缘有一个小的钝形刻痕。此时的危险就是螺旋桨上的这个缺口（当前状况），风险是螺旋桨断裂。

9.3.2 Hazardous Attitudes and Antidotes

9.3.2 危险态度和对策

Being fit to fly depends on more than just a pilot's physical condition and recent experience. For example, attitude will affect the quality of decisions. Attitude is a motivational predisposition to respond to people, situations, or events in a given manner. Studies have identified five hazardous attitudes that can interfere with the ability to make sound decisions and exercise authority properly: anti-authority, impulsivity, invulnerability, macho, and resignation.

飞行员的身体状况和最近的经验并不足以确定他/她是否适合飞行。态度也会影响决策的质量。态度是人们对事物的评价和行为倾向。研究发现，有五种危险态度对飞行员决策判断有严重影响，它们是反权威、冲动、侥幸、逞能和屈从。

Hazardous attitudes contribute to poor pilot judgment. Recognition of hazardous thoughts is the first step toward neutralizing them. After recognizing a thought as hazardous, the pilot should label it as hazardous. Antidotes should be memorized for each of the hazardous attitudes so they automatically come to mind when needed.

危险态度会导致飞行员判断力变差。消除危险态度的第一步就是可以识别到某一种想法是危险的。在意识到某一想法是危险的之后，飞行员应该将其标记为危险。飞行员应该记住每一种危险态度相对应的对策，以便在需要时它们能自动浮现在脑海中。

Anti-Authority: "Don't tell me."

This attitude is found in people who do not like anyone telling them what to do. They may be resentful of having someone tell them what to do, or may regard rules, regulations, and procedures as silly or unnecessary.

反权威："别告诉我该怎么做。"

这种态度存在于那些不喜欢别人告诉他们该做什么的人身上。他们可能对别人告诉他们该做什么感到不满，或者可能认为规则、规章和程序是愚蠢的或不必要的。

Impulsivity: "Do it quickly."

This is the attitude of people who frequently feel the need to do something, anything, immediately. They do not stop to think about what they are about to do; they do not select the best alternative, and they do the first thing that comes to mind.

冲动："快点做。"

经常感到时间紧迫，需要立刻做某事的人往往抱有这种态度。他们不会停下来想想他们要做什么；他们不会选择最好的备选方案，他们想到什么就做什么。

Invulnerability: "It won't happen to me."

Many people falsely believe that accidents happen to others, but never to them. They know accidents can happen, and they know that anyone can be affected. However, they never really feel or believe that they will be personally involved. Pilots who think this way are more likely to take chances.

侥幸："这不会发生在我身上。"

许多人错误地认为事故会发生在别人身上，但绝不会发生在自己身上。他们知道事故会发生，他们知道任何人都可能受到事故的影响。然而，他们从未真正感觉到或相信自己会亲身参与其中。有这样想法的飞行员更容易去冒险。

Macho: "I can do it."

Pilots who are always trying to prove that they are better than anyone else think, "I can do it—I'll show them." Pilots with this type of attitude will try to prove themselves by taking risks in order to impress others. While this pattern is thought to be a male characteristic, women are equally susceptible.

逞能："我能行。"

那些总想证明自己比别人强的飞行员，会想："我能行——我要证明给他们看。"有这种态度的飞行员会试图通过冒险来证明自己，并给别人留下深刻印象。男性和女性飞行员都可能会有这种危险态度。

Resignation: "What's the use?"

Pilots who think, "What's the use?" do not see themselves as being able to make a great deal of difference in what happens to them. When things go well, the pilot is apt to think that it is good luck. When things go badly, the pilot may feel that someone is out to get me, or attribute it to bad luck. Sometimes, such pilots will even go along with unreasonable requests just to be a "nice guy."

屈从："这有什么用?"

有这种想法的飞行员认为自己无法改变那些发生在自己身上的事情。当事情进展顺利时，他们会认为是运气使然。当事情进展不顺利时，他们可能会觉得有人要找自己麻烦，或者把这归咎于运气不好。有时候，他们甚至会为了做一个"好人"而接受一些不合理的要求。

Here are some antidotes.

对策如下。

NAME 危险情绪	DESCRIPTION 描述	ANTIDOTE 对策
Anti-authority 反权威	"Don't tell me..." 没人能告诉我该怎么做	Follow the rules; they're usually right. 严格遵守规则：规则通常是正确的
Impulsivity 冲动	"Do it quickly!" 任何事情都必须要速战速决	Not so fast-Think first! 不要急于下手，在没有想清楚之前不要急于着手做事情
Invulnerability 侥幸	"It won't happen to me..." "这不会发生在我身上"	It could happen to me! 这可能发生在我身上
Macho 逞能	"I can do it." "我当然能做到"	Taking chances is foolish. 冒险是极其愚蠢的
Resignation 屈从	"What's the use?" "做这些没有用"	I'm not helpless. 我不是无能为力

Lesson 10　ADM Process and Relevant Models
第 10 课　决策过程及相关模型

Three models of a structured framework for problem-solving and decision-making are the 5P, the 3P using PAVE, CARE, and TEAM, and the DECIDE models.

本节中将讲解在判断与决策中会使用到的 3 种模型，分别是 5P 模型、3P 模型（涉及 PAVE、CARE、TEAM 等检查单）及 DECIDE 模型。

10.1　Single-Pilot Resource Management (SRM)
10.1　单人制机组资源管理

October 2013, Department of Flight Standards, Civil Aviation Administration of China has issued New versions of the Private Pilot Practice Test Standard (Aircraft) (FS-PTS-001R1), Commercial Pilot Practice Test Standard (Aircraft) (FS-PTS-003R1) and Instrument Rating Practice Test Standard (FS-PTS-005R1). One of the most important changes is the addition of an assessment of Single-Pilot Resource Management (SRM) capabilities. SRM is the application of the concept of Crew Resource Management (CRM) in the operating environment of single Crew. The goal is to reduce human-induced accidents in general aviation by educating pilots about their limitations and how to improve their performance.

2013 年 10 月，中国民用航空局飞行标准司相继颁发了新版《私用驾驶员实践考试标准（飞机）》（FS-PTS-001R1）、《商用驾驶员实践考试标准（飞机）》（FS-PTS-003R1）和《仪表等级实践考试标准（飞机、直升机）》（FS-PTS-005R1）。一个重要的变化就是增加了针对单人制机组资源管理（Single Pilot Resource Management, SRM）能力的评估。SRM 是机组资源管理（Crew Resource Management, CRM）概念在单人制机组运行环境中的应用。其目的是通过向飞行员介绍个人能力局限以及如何提高个人能力表现，进而减少人为因素导致的通用航空飞行事故发生的概率。

SRM training is similar to CRM training in terms of methods and content, but the main difference is that SRM does not include training among flight crews (such as crew communication, leadership and cooperation, etc.). SRM training should begin with the pilot's initial training and continue throughout his or her flying career. SRM capabilities require continuous understanding and use by pilots on a daily basis to gradually be acquired. One of these practices is called the "5P" check pattern. The 5Ps consist of a Plan, a Plane, a Pilot, Passengers and Programming.

SRM 训练与 CRM 训练方式和内容比较类似，主要区别在于 SRM 不包含关于飞行机组之间的训练（例如机组交流、领导力与协作力等）。SRM 训练应从飞行员初始训练开始，并贯穿整个飞行生涯。SRM 能力需要飞行员在日常飞行中不断理解和使用才能逐渐获得。其中的一种练习方法称为“5P”检查模式。“5P”由计划（Plan）、飞机（Plane）、飞行员（Pilot）、乘客（Passengers）以及程序（Programming）组成。

10.2 The Plan, Plane, Pilot, Passengers, and Programming (5P) Model
10.2 5P 模型

Let's look at a detailed discussion of each of the 5Ps.

我们一同来详细讨论一下这个 5P 模型。

The Plan:

Flight planning results in not just a flight plan but familiarization of all events that surround the flight, The flight plan consists of the basic elements of cross-country planning, weather, route, fuel, etc. However, no matter how perfect the plan, external factors such as weather and aircraft status are subject to change at any time. It is for any number of factors that can impact the flight that the "Plan" should be reviewed and updated throughout the flight.

飞行计划:

飞行计划除了制订出飞行计划本身以外，飞行员还需要熟悉与飞行相关的所有事件。飞行计划包括转场计划、天气、航路、燃油等基本要素。然而，无论计划多么完美，天气、飞机状况等外部因素随时都可能发生变化。针对任何可能影响飞行的因素，“飞行计划”在整个飞行过程中都应该进行回顾和更新。

The Plane:

The "plane" consists of the usual array of mechanical and cosmetic issues that every aircraft pilot, owner, or operator can identify. With the advent of advanced avionics, the "plane" has expanded to include database, automation status, and emergency backup systems that were unknown a few years ago.

飞机:

“飞机”包括了飞机的机械特征及气动布局。随着先进航空电子设备的出现，“飞机”的内涵已经扩展到包括数据库、自动化状态和紧急情况下的备份系统。

The Pilot:

Flying, especially when business transportation is involved, can expose a pilot to risks such as high altitudes, long trips requiring significant endurance, and challenging weather. Advanced avionics, when installed, can expose a pilot to high stresses because of the inherent additional capabilities which are available. When dealing with pilot risk, it is always best to consult the "IMSAFE" checklist (as shown in Figure 10-1). The combination of late nights, pilot fatigue, and the effects of sustained flight above 5000 feet may cause pilots to become less discerning, less critical of information, less decisive, and more compliant and accepting. The 5P process helps a pilot recognize the physiological challenges that they may face towards the end of the flight before takeoff and allows them to update personal conditions as the flight progresses. Once risks are identified, the pilot is in a better place to make alternate plans that lessen the effect of these factors and provide a safer solution.

飞行员：

航线飞行员在飞行中常常面对高风险，如高海拔、长途飞行和边缘天气。安装先进的航空电子设备后，由于设备自身固有的附加功能，飞行员可能会承受更大的压力。在飞行风险出现时，飞行员要执行“IMSAFE”检查单（见图 10-1）确认自己的状态。熬夜、飞行员疲劳以及在 5000 英尺以上持续飞行的影响可能会导致飞行员的洞察力下降，对信息的处理能力降低，决策力下降，而更加屈从和接受现状。5P 模型帮助飞行员认识到他们在飞行结束前可能面临的挑战，并允许他们在飞行过程中不断更新个人状况。一旦确定了风险，飞行员就可以更好地制订备用计划，减少不利因素的影响，为飞行提供更安全的解决方案。

Are You Fit to Fly?
The "I'M SAFE" Checklist

I	llness?	Do I have any symptoms?
M	edication?	Have I been taking prescription or over-the-counter drugs?
S	tress?	Am I under psychological pressure form the job? Worried about financial matters, health problems or family discord?
A	lcohol?	Have I been drinking within eight hours? Within 24 hours?
F	atigue?	Am I tired and not adequately rested?
E	ating?	Am I adequately nourished?

Figure 10-1　I'M SAFE checklist

你是否适合飞行？
IMSAFE检查单

Illness(疾病)——我有什么症状吗？
Medication(药物)——我长期服用处方药或非处方药吗？
Stress(压力)——我有工作上的压力吗？担心经济问题、健康问题或家庭不和睦？
Alcohol(酒精)——我在8小时之内饮酒了吗？24小时之内呢？
Fatigue(疲劳)——我累吗？是不是休息不足？
Eating(饮食)——饮食营养均衡吗？

图 10-1　I'M SAFE 检查单

The Passengers:

If the passengers are not comfortable with a factual description of the risks present, then a good decision has generally been made. This discussion also allows the pilot to move past what they think the passengers want to do and find out what they want to do. This removes self-induced pressure from the pilot.

乘客：

如果乘客对当前面临风险的事实描述感到不舒服，这个时候就该好好做一个飞行决策了。飞行员不再为他们自认为的乘客的需求而困扰，而是去考虑乘客真实想法，这样也在一定程度上减少了飞行员的压力。

The Programming：

The electronic instrument displays, GPS, and autopilot reduce pilot workload and increase pilot situational awareness. While programming and operation of these devices are fairly simple and straightforward, unlike the analog instruments they replace, they tend to capture the pilot's attention and hold it for long periods of time. To avoid this phenomenon, the pilot should plan in advance when and where the programming for approaches, route changes, and airport information gathering should be accomplished, as well as times it should not. Pilot familiarity with the equipment, the route, the local ATC environment, and personal capabilities vis-ὰ-vis the automation should drive when, where, and how the automation is programmed and used.

程序：

在数字化仪表、GPS 以及自动驾驶仪的帮助下，飞行员减轻了工作负荷，提高了情景意识。这些设备与过去的设备相比，其操作及程序相对比较简单容易，但是却需要占用飞行员大量的时间和精力。为了避免这种现象，就要求飞行员事先完成进近程序的计划、航路的变化以及机场信息的搜集等工作。这些工作，包括熟悉设备、路线、目的机场的交通管制情况，以及能够知道何时、何地、如何使用自动驾驶等。

10.3　Perceive, Process, Perform (3P) Model
10.3　感知、处理、执行（3P）模型

The Perceive, Process, Perform (3P) model for ADM offers a simple, practical, and systematic approach applicable during all phases of flight. To use it, the pilot will:

(1) Perceive the given set of circumstances for a flight.

(2) Process by evaluating their impact on flight safety.

(3) Perform by implementing the best course of action.

决策中的感知、处理、执行（3P）模型提供了一种适用于飞行的各个阶段的简单、实用、系统的方法。要使用它，飞行员应：

(1) 感知：飞行的特定环境。

(2) 处理：评估它们对飞行安全的影响。

(3) 执行：实施最好的行动方案。

Depending upon the nature of the activity and the time available, risk management processing can occur in any of three timeframes. Most flight training activities happen in the "time-critical" timeframe for risk management. The 3P model combines six risk management steps for practical risk management: Perceive, Process, Perform with the PAVE, CARE, and

TEAM checklists. Pilots can help perceive hazards by using the PAVE checklist of Pilot, Aircraft, enVironment, and External pressures. They can process hazards using the CARE checklist of Consequences, Alternatives, Reality, External factors. Finally, pilots can perform risk management by using the TEAM choice list of Transfer, Eliminate, Accept, or Mitigate.

根据活动的性质和可用的时间，风险管理处理可以在三个时间中的任何一个时间发生。大多数飞行训练活动发生在风险管理的“关键”时段。3P 模型结合六个风险管理步骤用于实际的风险管理：感知、过程、执行与 PAVE、CARE 和 TEAM 清单。飞行员可以通过执行 PAVE 检查单来感知来自飞行员、飞机、环境和外部压力带来的安全威胁。他们可以执行 CARE 检查单，通过评估后果、制定备选方案、结合现实、外部因素处理危险。最后，飞行员可以通过执行 TEAM 检查单来转移、消除、接受或减轻风险从而进行风险管理。

10.3.1 Risk Management

10.3.1 风险管理

What is risk management? Risk management is a decision-making process designed to systematically identify hazards, assess the degree of risk, and determine the best course of action. A few definitions:

什么是风险管理？风险管理是一个决策过程，旨在系统地识别危险，评估风险程度，并确定最佳行动方案。一些定义如下：

- A hazard is a present condition, event, object, or circumstance that could lead to or contribute to an unplanned or undesired event. For example, a nick in the propeller represents a hazard.
- Risk is the future impact of a hazard that is not controlled or eliminated.
- 危险：可能导致或促成非计划事件或意外事件出现的现状、事件、对象或情景。例如，螺旋桨上出现裂口就是飞行中的危险情况。
- 风险：危险没有控制或消除的情况下会产生的影响。

Assessment of risk is an important part of good ADM. The hazard described above——a nick in the propeller——poses a risk only if the airplane is flown. If the damaged propeller is exposed to the constant vibration of normal engine operation, there is a high risk is that it could fracture and cause catastrophic damage to the engine and/or airframe (not to mention the occupants of the aircraft!).

风险评估是良好决策的重要组成部分。上述危险——螺旋桨上的裂口——只有在飞机飞行时才构成风险。发动机正常运行，受损的螺旋桨在持续振动下很有可能断裂，并对发动机和/或机身造成致命损伤（同样威胁到机上乘客安全）。

As you work through the ADM cycle, especially the "process" step in which you analyze the information you have perceived in preparation for the "perform" step, it might help you to remember the four fundamental principles of risk management.

进行决策时，尤其是处在 3P 模式中的“处理”阶段，飞行员已经分析了所有感知的信息，正在为“执行”做准备，请记住以下四个处理风险管理的基本原则。

(1) Accept no unnecessary risk. Flying is not possible without risk, but unnecessary risk comes without a corresponding return. If you are flying a new airplane for the first time, you might

determine that the risk of making that flight in low IFR conditions is unnecessary.

(1) 不接受不必要的风险。飞行不可能没有风险，但不要为了那些不必要的风险去冒险。如果您是初次驾驶飞机，没有必要冒险在低仪表飞行条件下飞行。

(2) Make risk decisions at the appropriate level. Risk decisions should be made by the person who can develop and implement risk controls. Remember that you are pilot-in-command, so never let anyone else—not ATC and not your passengers—make risk decisions for you.

(2) 风险决策应由机长做出。风险决策应由能够实施风险控制的人员做出。请记住，机长是决策者，不要让空管人员、乘客做风险决策。

(3) Accept risk when benefits outweigh dangers (costs). In any flying activity, it will be necessary to accept some degree of risk. A day with good weather, for example, is a much better time to fly an unfamiliar airplane for the first time than a day with low IFR conditions.

(3) 当利好大于危险（成本）时，可以接受风险。在任何飞行活动中，都必须接受一定程度的风险。例如，您初次驾驶不熟悉的飞机时，应选择好天气，而不是选择低能见度的仪表飞行条件下飞行。

(4) Integrate risk management into planning at all levels. Because risk is an unavoidable part of every flight, safety requires the use of appropriate and effective risk management not just in the preflight planning stage, but in all stages of the flight.

(4) 将风险管理纳入飞行的每一个阶段。由于风险是每一次飞行不可避免的一部分,我们不仅在飞行前计划阶段应该做风险管理,在飞行的所有阶段都应采用适当和有效的风险管理。

10.3.2 Perceive

10.3.2 感知

At any given moment, information affecting the outcome of a flight is all around you. How you manage that flow of information will definitely have an effect on the relative success or failure of each and every flight. First, gather information from all available sources. You will want to perceive situations or facts related to each major element of your flight:

- Pilot, passengers, and other people involved.
- Aircraft you will be flying.
- enVironment in which you will operate (e. g., airport, airspace, weather).
- External pressures likely to influence your decision-making process.

在任何特定的时刻，您都身处在影响飞行的因素之中。如何管理信息肯定会影响到每一次飞行的结果。首先，需要从所有可用来源中收集信息。您需要了解以下与航班要素相关的情况或事实，比如：

- 飞行员、乘客和其他相关人员。
- 您将驾驶的飞机。
- 您将运行的环境（例如，机场、空域、天气）。
- 可能影响您决策过程的外部压力。

PAVE Checklist (as shown in Figure 10-2): Identify Hazards and Personal Minimums:

这里就涉及一个 PAVE 检查单（见图 10-2），我们用这个检查单来辨别危险和个人最低安全标准。

PILOT

Experience/Recency
- Takeoffs/landings.................. ______ in the last ______ days
- Hours in make/model........... ______ in the last ______ days
- Instrument approaches (simulated or actual)........... ______ in the last ______ days
- Instrument flight hours (simulated or actual).......... ______ in the last ______ days
- Terrain and airspace.......................... familiar

Physical Condition
- Sleep...................................... ______ in the last 24 hours
- Food and water..................... in the last ______ hours
- Alcohol................................ None in the last ______ hours
- Drugs or medication............ None in the last ______ hours
- Stressful events.................... None in the last ______ days
- Illnesses................................ None in the last ______ days

▶ ______

AIRCRAFT

Fuel Reserves(Cross-Country)
- VFR Day................................ ______ hours
- Night.............................. ______ hours
- IFR Day................................. ______ hours
- Night.............................. ______ hours

Experience in Type
- Takeoffs/landings in aircraft type.................. ______ in the last ______ days

Aircraft Performance

Establish that you have additional performance available over that required. Consider the following:
- Gross weight
- Load distribution
- Density altitude
- Performance charts

Aircraft Equipment
- Avionics............... familiar with equipment (including autopilot and GPS systems)
- COM/NAV............ equipment appropriate to flight
- Charts................... current
- Clothing................ suitable for preflight and flight
- Survival gear......... appropriate for flight/terrain

▶ ______

ENVIRONMENT

Airport Conditions
- Crosswind................ ______ % of max POH
- Runway length.......... ______ % more than POH

Weather
- Reports and forecasts.................. not more than ______ hours old
- Icing conditions.................. within aircraft/pilot capabilities

Weather for VFR
- Ceiling Day............................. ______ feet
- Night......................... ______ feet
- Visibility Day.......................... ______ miles
- Night......................... ______ miles

Weather For IFR
- Precision Approaches
  - Ceiling................. ______ feet above min.
  - Visibility.............. ______ mile(s) above min.
- Non-Precision Approaches
  - Ceiling................. ______ feet above min.
  - Visibility.............. ______ mile(s) above min.
- Missed Approaches
  - No more than........ ______ before diverting
- Takeoff Minimums
  - Ceiling................. ______ feet
  - Visibility.............. ______ mile(s)

▶ ______

EXTERNAL PRESSURES

Trip Planning
- Allowance for delays.......... ______ minutes

Diversion or Cancellation Aitemate Plans
- Notification of person(s) you are meeting
- Passengers briefed on diversion or cancellation plans and alternatives
- Modiflcation or cancellation of car rental，restaurant，or hotel reservations
- Arrangement of alternative transportation (alrline, car, etc.)

Personal Equlpment
- Credit card and telephone numbers available for alternate plans
- Approprlate clothing or personal needs(eye wear，medication...) in the event of an unexpected stay

▶ ______

Figure 10-2　PAVE checklist

飞行员	飞机	环境	外部压力
经验/最近飞行情况： 起飞/着陆 ____最近几天真实飞行/模拟机飞行 ____最近几天 仪表进近 （模拟器/真实飞行） ____最近几天 仪表飞行小时数 （模拟器/真实飞行） ____最近几天 地形和空域-熟悉 身体情况： 睡眠____ ____最近 24 小时 食物和水 最近____小时 酒精 最近____小时内未饮酒 麻醉药和其他药品 最近____小时内未用药 压力事件 最近____天内未出现 生病 最近____天内未生病	所剩燃油（转场）目视飞行 白天____小时 夜晚____小时 该机型的飞行经历 该机型的起飞/着陆 ____最近几天 机型性能 你应该了解更多的机型性能数据，比如下述： 总重 负载分类 密度高度 性能图表 飞机设备： 机载设备：熟悉（自动驾驶，GPS） 通信/导航：设备可用航图：最新的 外蒙皮：适于飞行 起落架：适于飞行/地形	机场 侧风最大值的____%跑道长度超过最大值的____% 天气 气象报文不超过____小时前 结冰情况____飞机/飞行员接受范围内 目视飞行天气 云高 白天____英尺 夜间____英尺 能见度 白天____英里 夜间____英里 仪表飞行天气 精密进近 云高 超过最低限度 ____英尺 能见度 超过最低限度 ____英里 非精密进近 云高 超过最低限度 ____英尺 能见度 超过最低限度 ____英里 起飞最低限制 云高____英尺 能见度____英里	飞行计划 允许延误____分钟 备选方案 通知你要会见的人 向乘客介绍改航或取消航班的计划和备选方案 更改或取消汽车租赁、餐厅或酒店预订 安排替代交通工具（航空公司、汽车）等 个人设备 有效的支付和通信方式 适当的服装或个人物品（眼罩、药物……）以防非预期入住酒店

图 10-2 PAVE 检查单

All four elements combine and interact to create a unique situation for any flight. Pay special attention to the pilot aircraft combination, and consider whether the combined "pilot—aircraft team" is capable of the mission you want to fly. For example, you may have a new technically advanced aircraft with moving map GPS, weather data link, and autopilot—but if you do not have much weather flying experience or practice in using this kind of equipment, you cannot rely on the airplane's capability to compensate for limited experience.

这四种元素结合并相互作用，创造出一个独特的飞行环境。特别关注飞行员与飞机的组合，考虑组合后的“飞行员—飞机”组合是否能够完成飞行任务。例如飞机装有实时定位 GPS，天气上传数据链，以及自动驾驶——但如果飞行员没有太多在恶劣天气中的飞行经验或不熟悉先进设备的使用，飞行员就无法依靠飞机的设备来弥补飞行经验的不足。

10.3.3 Process

10.3.3 处理

The second part is to process the information that you perceived in step one. As you receive information, it is filtered through the five senses: sight, hearing, smell, touch, and taste. In this step, however, the goal is to organize the information, interpret it, and try to match the alternatives with situations from your experience. To analyze in a structured way, process with CARE:

- Consequences of each hazard associated with the PAVE elements.
- Alternatives available.
- Reality of the situation or hazard.
- External pressures that might influence your analysis.

第二部分是处理飞行员在第一步中感知到的信息。在飞行员接收信息的时候，它通过五种感官进行过滤：视觉、听觉、嗅觉、触觉和味觉。“处理”信息的目标是组织信息、解释信息，并尝试根据飞行员的经验选择对应的备选方案。要以结构化方式进行信息分析，可使用 CARE 检查单。

- PAVE 模型中的元素相关的每种危害后果。
- 可用的备选方案。
- 实际情况或现实危险。
- 可能影响您分析的外部压力。

CARE Checklist: Review Hazards and Evaluate Risks

CARE 检查单：检查危险并评估风险

In the second step, the goal is to process this information to evaluate their impact on the safety of your flight and consider, "why must I CARE about these circumstances?"

对于 3P 模式来说，第二步的目标是对信息的处理，目的是评估它们对飞行安全的影响，并考虑“为什么我必须 CARE（在意）这些情况？”

For each hazard that you perceived in step one, use the CARE checklist of Consequences,

Alternatives, Reality, External factors. For example, let's evaluate a night flight to attend a business meeting。

对于在第一步中察觉到的每一种危险，执行 CARE 检查单。例如，评估一次乘坐夜间航班参加商务会议的飞行。

Consequences: departing after a full workday creates fatigue and pressure.

Alternatives: delay until morning; reschedule meeting; drive.

Reality: dangers, and distractions of fatigue could lead to an accident.

External pressures: business meeting at the destination might influence me.

后果：在工作了一整天后起飞会造成疲劳和压力。

备选方案：天亮再出发；重新安排会议；开车前往。

现实：因疲劳带来的注意力分散可能会导致飞行事故。

外部压力：这次商务会议可能会影响到我的职业发展。

A good rule of thumb for the processing phase: if you find yourself saying that it will "probably" be okay, it is time for a solid reality check. If you are worried about missing a meeting, be realistic about how that pressure will affect not just your initial go/no-go decision but also your inflight decisions to continue the flight or divert.

对于第二个步骤，即处理阶段，有一个很好的经验法则：如果您认为这种操作“可能”是好的，就应该对此进行一次检查。如果你担心错过会议，那么要现实地考虑，因为压力不仅会影响你最初的决定，即去还是不去，还会影响你飞行中的继续飞行或改航的决定。

10.3.4 Perform

10.3.4 执行

Now it is time to act, which leads to the third part of the process: perform. How you act—perform—will be based on the perceiving and processing you did in the first two steps. At the most basic level, you perform in one of two ways: action or inaction. As you noticed in the perceive and process steps, there are a lot of external pressures on the human decision-making process. These influences may directly or indirectly affect the action or inaction you choose and also affect how quickly and decisively you perform. In the perform step, you need to do one of the following:

- Mitigate the hazard(s) and risk that you perceived and processed.
- Eliminate the hazard(s) and risk that you perceived and processed.

现在是采取行动的时候了，也就是 3P 模型中的最后一步：执行。您的执行行为取决于您在前两个步骤中所做的对信息的感知和对信息的处理。这个执行也就是您的作为或不作为。正如您在感知和处理步骤中所注意到的，人类决策过程受到大量的外部压力的影响。这些影响可能直接或间接影响您选择的作为或不作为，也可能影响您执行的速度和果断程度。在执行步骤中，您需要执行以下操作之一：

- 缓解您感知和处理的各种危险和风险。
- 消除您感知和处理的各种危险和风险。

The TEAM checklist can be applied to manage the risk control better.

此时，我们可以使用 TEAM 检查单帮助我们更好地控制风险。

TEAM Checklist: Choose and Implement Risk Controls

Perform risk management by using the TEAM checklist of Transfer, Eliminate, Accept, Mitigate to deal with each factor:

Transfer—Should this risk decision be transferred to someone else (e. g., do you need to consult the chief flight instructor?)

Eliminate—Is there a way to eliminate the hazard?

Accept—Do the benefits of accepting risk outweigh the costs?

Mitigate—What can you do to mitigate the risk?

TEAM 检查单：选择并执行风险控制

使用 TEAM 检查单中的“转移、消除、接受及缓解”进行风险管理，并处理每个风险因素：

转移——是否将此风险决策权转移给其他人（例如，你是否需要咨询飞行教官？）

消除——有消除危险的方法吗？

接受——接受风险的结果是利大于弊吗？

缓解——为了减轻风险，你能做些什么？

The goal is to perform by eliminating hazards or mitigating risk and then continuously evaluating this action's outcome. With the example of low ceilings at the destination, the pilot can perform good ADM by selecting a suitable alternate, knowing where to find good weather, and carrying sufficient fuel to reach it. This course of action would mitigate the risk. The pilot also has the option to eliminate it by waiting for better weather.

执行 TEAM 检查单，飞行员完成了消除危险或降低风险，持续评估。以目的地的低云天气为例，飞行员可以通过选择合适的备降场制定一个良好的决策，找到气象条件好的机场，携带足够的燃油到达目的地，这种决策就是在减轻风险。飞行员还可以选择等待天气变好后再飞行，这样做就是在消除风险。

10.4 How to Improve Your ADM: DECIDE Model
10.4 如何提高你的决策能力：DECIDE 模式

Using the acronym "DECIDE" the six-step process DECIDE Model is another continuous loop process that provides the pilot with a logical way of making decisions. DECIDE means to Detect, Estimate, Choose a course of action, Identify solutions, Do the necessary actions, and Evaluate the effects of the actions. In order to learn the DECIDE model better, here is a case for analysis.

DECIDE 模型使用了以下六个单词 Detect（觉察）、Estimate（估计）、Choose（选择）、Identify（鉴别）、Do（实施）、Evaluate（评价）的首字母缩写，决策者发现“变化已经发生了的事实”，估计“应对变化的需求”，选择“一个令人满意的结果”，确定“能成功应对变化的行动方案”，采取“必要的行动”，评价“采取的行动方案的效果”。

为了能够更好地学习 DECIDE 模型，我们引入一个案例进行分析。

Now let's use DECIDE model to check out how the crew made the decision.

现在让我们看看如何用 DECIDE 模型去分析机组的决策。

Flight 3U8633, operated by Sichuan Airlines, prepares to conduct emergency landing after a mechanical failure in Chengdu Shuangliu International Airport in Chengdu, capital of Southwest China's Sichuan province, May 14, 2018.

The windshield on the co-pilot side in the cockpit shattered at a cruising altitude of 32000 feet. As the windshield broke and blew out, the cockpit lost pressure, with the co-pilot nearly sucked out from the plane with only his seat belt saving him. The accident made the equipment malfunction and the flight went into a nosedive that lasted five to six seconds. Facing low temperature of minus 40 degree Celsius, tearing wind of 800～900km/h, and deafening sound, the pilot grabbed a oxygen mask and manually controlled the plane, displaying extraordinary professionalism and will power. The pilot heroically saved more than 100 passengers and crew members on the flight.

2018 年 5 月 14 日，四川航空 3U8633 航班发生机械故障，在成都双流国际机场紧急降落。

在 32000 英尺的巡航高度，驾驶舱内副驾驶一侧的挡风玻璃破裂。当挡风玻璃破裂时，驾驶舱失压，副驾驶几乎被吸出了飞机，仅有安全带固定住他。事故导致设备出现故障，飞行高度骤降持续了 5～6s。在−40℃的低温、风速 800～900km/h、震耳欲聋的声音中，飞行员抓住氧气面罩，用手操纵飞机，表现出了非凡的专业性和意志力。飞行员的英勇行为拯救了飞机上 100 多名乘客和机组人员。

Detect (the Problem)

Problem detection is the first step in the decision-making process. It begins with recognizing a change occurred or an expected change did not occur. A problem is perceived first by the senses and then it is distinguished through insight and experience. In this case, the Captain Liu detected that the windshield on the co-pilot side in the cockpit shattered.

觉察（问题）

觉察到问题是决策过程中的第一步，它始于认识到飞行中发生了变化，或者预期会出现的变化没有发生。飞行员通过感官感知到变化，然后通过自身的洞察力和经验来区分变化。在本案例中，川航 8633 刘机长发现了右侧挡风玻璃破裂，就是察觉到了变化。

Estimate (the Need To React)

For example, what if the cabin door of an aircraft suddenly opened in flight while the aircraft climbed through 1500 feet on a clear sunny day? In fact, the door's opening would not impact safe flight and can almost be disregarded. Most likely, a pilot would return to the airport to secure the door after landing. The pilot flying on a clear day faced with this minor problem may rank the open cabin door as a low risk. What about the pilot on an IFR climb out in IMC conditions with light intermittent turbulence in rain who is receiving an amended clearance from air traffic control (ATC)? The open cabin door now becomes a higher risk factor. The problem has not changed, but the perception of risk a pilot assigns it changes because of the multitude of ongoing tasks and the environment. Experience, discipline, awareness, and knowledge will influence how a pilot ranks a problem.

估计（应对的需要）

在一个阳光明媚的日子里，飞机爬升到 1500 英尺的高度时，飞机的客舱门突然打开了，该怎么办？事实上，此时客舱门的打开不会在很大程度上影响安全飞行。很可能的解决办法是返回机场，着陆后检查舱门安全。在晴朗的天气飞行的飞行员遇到这个小问题，可能会将这个打开的客舱门列为低风险项目。但是如果在仪表气象条件下、雨中有轻度间歇性湍流、飞行员在爬升阶段正在接收空中交通管制的重新许可，在这样的情景下，敞开的舱门就成了一个更高的风险因素。问题本身并没有改变，但是飞行员对风险的感知会随着正在进行的任务和环境的改变而改变。经验、条例、意识和知识都将影响飞行员对某个问题的排序。

In this case, the crew of Flight 3U8633 estimated the factors such as the cabin depressurization, partial damage to cockpit equipment, co-pilot incapacitation, 40 degrees Celsius below zero, high winds.

在本案例中，客舱失压、驾驶舱部分设备受损、副驾驶失能、气温-40℃、大风都是需要机组进行估计的因素。

Choose (a Course of Action)

After the problem has been identified and its impact estimated, the pilot must determine the desirable outcome and choose a course of action. In the case of the multi engine pilot given the simulated failed engine, the desired objective is to safely land the airplane.

选择（行动方案）

确定问题、对其影响做出估计之后，飞行员必须确定事态发展的理想结果并选择行动方式。如果模拟多引擎飞机引擎故障的特情，飞行员选择的最理想的结果就是飞机能够安全着陆。

In this case, the crew declared the emergency situation.

在本案例中，机组宣布了紧急情况。

Identify (Solutions)

The pilot formulates a plan that will take him or her to the objective. Sometimes, there may be only one course of action available. In this case, the crew conducted emergency landing after a mechanical failure in Chengdu Shuangliu International Airport in Chengdu.

确定（解决方案）

为了实现目标，飞行员制订计划。有时，计划只是一种可行的行动方案。在本案例中，机组返回成都双流机场迫降。

Do (the Necessary Actions)

Once pathways to resolution are identified, the pilot selects the most suitable one for the situation.

采取（行动）

一旦确定了解决方案，飞行员就会根据实际情况选择最合适的路径。

In this case, the crew adopted the action of captain controlling, communicating with the co-pilot by gesture, spiral down and reducing the flight speed appropriately.

在本案例中，机组采取机长操纵，并与副驾驶用手势交流，盘旋下降高度，适当降低飞行速度的行动方案。

Evaluate (the Effect of the Action)

Finally, after implementing a solution, evaluate the decision to see if it was correct. If the action taken does not provide the desired results, the process may have to be repeated. In this case, the crew controlled the airplane to get landed safely.

评估（行动的效果）

最后，在执行一个解决方案之后，评估这个决策方案，看看它是否正确。如果所采取的行动不能实现预期的结果，再做新一轮决策。本案例中，评估结果为飞机可控，安全落地。

Lesson 11　Case Study：Judge and ADM Errors
第 11 课　案例分析：判断和决策错误

Pilot mistakes are often called "pilot error", formally defined as: An action or inaction that leads to a deviation from intentions and expectations. Sometimes, pilot error involves deficiencies in aircraft control skill. Examples might include turning the wrong knob on the GPS navigator. Use of aircraft training devices, computer-based training, and regular practice in the aircraft can help prevent these errors.

飞行员所犯的错误通常被称为“飞行员差错”，定义：飞行员的做法或是不作为导致偏离意图和期望的结果。有时，飞行员的失误涉及飞机控制技能方面的缺陷。比如转错导航面板上的旋钮等。使用飞机训练设备、基于计算机的训练以及定期在飞机上练习有助于防止这些错误。

Let's go back to the example mentioned at the very beginning of this chapter.

我们回到本章开头的案例。

By discussing the events that led to this accident, it can be understood how a series of judgmental errors contributed to the final outcome of this flight. For example, one of the first elements that affected the pilot's flight was fatigue. The pilot understood that fatigue and hunger could affect the ability to fly safely, but let the desire to stay on schedule override the concern for a safe flight.

通过讨论导致这次事故的事件，可以理解一系列判断错误是如何导致这次飞行的最终结果的。例如，影响飞行员飞行的首要因素之一是疲劳。飞行员明白疲劳和饥饿可能会影响安全飞行的能力，但却让按计划飞行的愿望压倒了对安全飞行的关注。

Next, the rush to get airborne led the pilot to skip or postpone necessary aspects of preflight planning. Research before takeoff, with a quick review before descent, could have ensured a clear mental picture of the location of the airport in relation to the town.

接下来，仓促起飞导致飞行员跳过了飞行前计划的必要环节：起飞前准备，以及下降前的快速回顾，这些可以确保飞行员在头脑中形成以一个机场与城镇相对位置的清晰印象。

Copying relevant information from flight guides and other information sources is part of careful preflight planning. Studying the aeronautical charts and checking the Notices to Airmen (NOTAM) before hand would have alerted the pilot to towers, terrain, and other obstructions in the vicinity of the airport. Even without proper planning before the flight, good cockpit resource management and organization would have had the flight guide and any other necessary information near at hand. Approaching the airport environment and flying around the area at traffic pattern altitude in hazy conditions could have interfered with other air traffic, and the potential for a midair collision is obvious.

飞行计划中很重要的一部分是从飞行指南和其他信息来源获取相关信息。事先研究航图和查看飞行员通告（NOTAM），可以提醒飞行员注意机场附近的塔台、地形和其他障碍物。即使在飞行前没有适当的计划，良好的驾驶舱资源管理和组织也会使飞行指南和任何其他必要的信息近在咫尺。在雾霾条件下接近机场并在起落航线高度上盘旋，可能会干扰其他空中交通，而发生空中碰撞的可能性是显而易见的。

In all circumstances, the pilot's first duty is to fly the airplane. Clearly that would include adjusting the power, setting the trim, and keeping track of altitude. This pilot was extremely fortunate—the outcome could easily have been fatal. On numerous occasions during the flight, the pilot could have made effective decisions that would have broken the chain of error and prevented this accident. Making sound decisions is the key to preventing accidents. Traditional pilot training has emphasized flying skills, knowledge of the airplane, and familiarity with regulations. ADM training focuses on the decision-making process and the factors that affect a pilot's ability to make effective choices.

在任何情况下，飞行员的首要职责是驾驶飞机。显然，这将包括调整动力、设置配平，并保持高度。这位飞行员非常幸运，否则结果很可能是致命的。在飞行过程中，飞行员本可以做出有效的决定，打破错误链条，防止这次事故。做出正确的决定是预防事故的关键。传统的飞行员培训强调飞行技能、飞机知识和对法规的熟悉。ADM 培训关注决策过程和影响飞行员做出有效选择的因素。

Further Reading
ADM in Flight: Hero Captain of China's Civil Aviation
拓展阅读
空中决策：中国民航英雄机长

Reading 1

Plane Forced to Divert after Mechanical Failure
Xinhua

飞机因机械故障被迫备降
新华社

Flight 3U8633, operated by Sichuan Airlines, prepares to conduct emergency landing after a mechanical failure in Chengdu Shuangliu International Airport in Chengdu, capital of Southwest China's Sichuan province, May 14, 2018.

2018 年 5 月 14 日，四川航空公司 3U8633 航班遇到机械故障，在中国西南地区的四川省省会成都的双流国际机场准备进行紧急降落。

A Chinese commercial flight was forced to divert to an alternate airport after a mechanical failure, authorities confirmed Monday.

经官方周一证实，一架中国民航班机在出现机械故障后，被迫改航备降到另一机场。

Flight 3U8633, operated by Sichuan Airlines, was en route from Southwest China's Chongqing municipality to Lhasa, capital of Tibet autonomous region. It was forced to divert to Chengdu, capital of Sichuan province.

由四川航空公司运营的 3U8633 航班，执飞从中国西南部的重庆市到西藏自治区的首府拉萨的飞行任务，最后备降到四川省省会成都。

According to the Civil Aviation Administration of China (CAAC), part of the cockpit window broke as the Airbus A319 flew over Chengdu. The aircrew enacted emergency code 7700 and landed in Chengdu. All passengers are safe, although the co-pilot sustained injuries to the face and waist, and another crew member was slightly hurt during the emergency landing, according to the CAAC.

根据中国民航局透露，这架空客 A319 客机在成都上空飞行时驾驶舱风挡破裂。机组人员挂出了紧急代码 7700 并降落在成都。中国民航局称，所有乘客都平安，但副驾驶员的脸部和腰部受伤，另一名机组人员在紧急着陆时受了轻伤。

Sichuan Airlines confirmed the diversion, and said that an investigation is under way.

四川航空公司证实了这一消息，并表示正在进行调查。

There were 119 passengers and nine crew members on board, according to the airline, which has arranged another flight to take the passengers to Lhasa.

据该航空公司透露，飞机上有 119 名乘客和 9 名机组成员。公司已经安排另一架航班将乘客送往拉萨。

Video footage shot by passengers showed baggage falling from overhead lockers during the emergency landing and oxygen masks dropping for use.

根据乘客们拍摄的视频显示，在紧急着陆时，行李从行李架上掉了下来，氧气面罩脱落。

Reading 2

But the windshield later "shattered with a loud sound" the pilot, Liu Chuanjian, said in a video posted by the news outlet Chengdu Business News. "When I looked over to my side, half of my co-pilot's body was hanging out of the window."

但风挡玻璃随后“爆裂，‘哄’一声发出巨大的声响，”机长刘传健在新闻媒体《成都商报》发布的一段视频中说。“我往旁边看时，副驾驶（身体）已经飞出去一半，半边身体在窗外悬挂。”

"Fortunately, he was wearing a seatbelt," Mr. Liu said.

“还好，他系了安全带。”刘传建说。

The plane made an emergency landing at 7：42 am in the southwestern Chinese city of Chengdu.

飞机于上午 7 点 42 分在中国西南部的成都市紧急迫降。

Later on Monday, Sichuan Airlines said in a post on Weibo, China's Twitter-like microblogging platform, that 29 of the plane's 119 passengers were sent to a hospital for examination. One cabin crew member was being treated for a waist injury and the first officer suffered scratches, but the remaining passengers were discharged, the post said.

周一晚些时候，四川航空在新浪微博上发帖表示，机上的 119 名乘客中有 29 名被送往医院进行检查。帖子写道，一名乘务员腰部受伤，正在接受治疗。副驾驶皮肤擦伤。但其余乘客都已出院。

Many Chinese social media users lauded the pilots as heroes and encouraged the airline to reward them.

中国许多社交媒体用户赞扬飞行员们是英雄，并鼓励航空公司对他们进行奖励。

The glass on the right side of the cockpit suddenly burst. This led to the instantaneous loss of air pressure in the cabin, and the temperature instantly reduced to minus 30 degrees, and the cabin is facing the wind at the speed of 800km/h, the eardrum also produces severe pain because of the huge pressure difference...

驾驶舱右侧玻璃突然破裂导致机舱瞬间失压，温度瞬间降低到-30℃，舱内面临的是 800km/h 的狂风，耳膜也因为巨大的压强差产生剧痛……

In this extremely emergent situations, human consciousness can only last for one to two minutes.

在这种极其紧急的情况下，人的意识大概只能维持一到两分钟。

At the critical moment, Liu Chuanjian, the captain of the flight originating from the military, relying on 20 years of flight experience and manual maneuvers in the event of failure of automation equipment, succeeded in allowing the aircraft to prepare for Chengdu Shuangliu Airport and saved 119 passengers and 9 crew members.

危急关头，军人出身的航班机长刘传健在自动化设备失灵情况下，依靠二十年飞行经验，手动操纵，成功让飞机备降在了成都双流机场，挽救了 119 位乘客和 9 名机组人员的生命安全。

The two captains managed to turn the tide in half an hour. Experts in the civil aviation industry have always praised the successful landing of this plane as a miracle.

两位机长在半小时内力挽狂澜。民航业界的专家们也一直称赞本次飞机紧急降落成功是一个奇迹。

Let us praise the hero captain!

让我们为英雄机长点赞!

Flight Training Files
飞行训练档案

Case 1
案例 1

Xiao Ming will have his first flight at the flight school at seven o 'clock in the morning the next day. Because there are a lot of things to prepare for the first flight, the instructor asked him to go to school at six o ' clock for pre-flight preparation. That afternoon Xiao Ming and his classmates had milk tea to celebrate the coming maiden flight. After dinner, Xiao Ming went to bed at half past ten after playing computer games with his classmates, but he was too excited to fall asleep until one o 'clock in the morning. Xiao Ming threw up into a sick bag during the flight the next day.

小明第二天一早七点就要进行他在航校的第一班飞行，因为第一班飞行有很多准备的东西，所以教员让他六点就到航校进行航前准备。这一天下午小明与同学们一起点了奶茶庆祝即将到来的首飞。吃过晚饭后和同学们相约一起打游戏，十点半小明上床准备睡觉，但是由于太过激动直到凌晨一点才睡着。第二天的飞行中小明吐了一呕吐袋。

Briefing
讲评

The caffeine and theophylline in milk tea would keep Xiao Ming awake at night. Gaming before sleep makes him feel excited. It's not likely to fall asleep soon after that. Vomiting in the first flight due to physical or mental reasons is common. But we should adjust ourselves, getting enough sleep would effectively avoid vomiting.

下午奶茶中的咖啡因与茶碱会导致小明晚上睡不着，睡前的游戏让人兴奋，打完游戏后不太可能立刻睡着。首次飞行中由于身体或精神原因出现呕吐是很常见的，但是飞行前应调整好心态，获得充足的睡眠可以有效避免或减轻呕吐的症状。

Case 2
案例 2

After a period of flying alone, Xiao Ming had accumulated more than 100 hours of flying experience, and now he felt he was a mature pilot. So every time he did not check the plane carefully according to the daily inspection, and made a flight plan only in general. He only made correction about those errors that the instructor pointed out. Xiao Ming said: "it doesn't matter, every inspection and route are the same so I have nothing to worry about." Until one time, Xiao Ming started the plane and taxied without removing the pitot tube cover. He was then called back.

经过一段时间的单飞，小明已经积攒了一百多个小时的飞行经历，此时的他觉得自己已经是个成熟的飞行员了。所以每次他都不会按照检查单一项一项仔细地检查飞机，做飞行计划时也只做个大概，教员指出了他就改，教员不指出时他就企图蒙混过关。小明表示：没关系，每次的检查和路线都是一样的，有什么好担心的。直到有一次小明连皮托管套都没有摘就发动了飞机滑出了，被航校在跑道上召回。

Briefing
讲评

Here's the picture of a pitot tube (as shown in Figure 11-1). It provides pitot source. To prevent it being stuck, we usually put the cover on when we are not about to fly. Those covers are in fresh colors. And removing the covers is part of the items we should check before starting the engine. Even if you've entered solo phrase, don't take yourself seriously. It will be your own responsibility when you are going solo. Don't ask others to be your backup. Prepare well and stay humble.

图 11-1 为皮托管，可以提供动压源。为防止异物卡阻，我们通常在飞机不使用时套上皮托管套。皮托管套一般颜色鲜艳，是发动机启动前最后需要再次检查的项目之一。即使进入单飞，在这个阶段不能太把自己当回事。单飞时责任机长是自己，不能再依靠别人来给你做靠背，要做好自己的分内之事，做好每次航前准备工作，虚心学习。

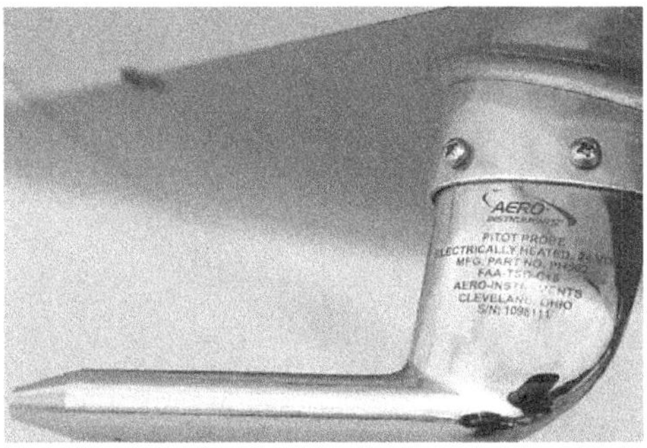

Figure 11-1　Pitot tube
图 11-1　皮托管

扫一扫查看彩图

Case 3
案例 3

Xiao Ming and his instructor were doing a XC（cross-country）. Shortly after taking off from the base airport, Xiao Ming talked to the instructor, but the instructor did not respond. Xiao Ming called him twice, but he still did not answer. Xiao Ming turned his head only to find the instructor fainted. If you were Xiao Ming, what should you do at this time?

小明和教员在飞一班转场，从基地机场起飞后不久小明与教员搭话，教员却没有回应。小明连续叫了两次教员都没有理睬。小明转头一看教员晕了过去。如果你是小明，这时你应该怎么办？

Briefing
讲评

Instructor out of consciousness is called incapacitation. Keeping calm at this moment, and make sure the flying condition is safe. Make a decision according to actual conditions. You can return to takeoff airport because you just took off before long. Or you can get to the nearest alternate. Then turn to ATC or school frequency for help. Remember Aviate-Navigate-Communicate!

教员失去意识属于空中失能，此时首先要保持冷静，保证飞机飞行状态安全。然后根据实际情况决断。由于刚从机场起飞不久，可以考虑返航或去最近的合适备降场。然后再联系 ATC 和航校汇报情况，寻求其他帮助。期间始终牢记 Aviate-Navigate-Communicate 的顺序。

Unit 5
Cockpit Leadership

第 5 篇　驾驶舱领导

Lead-in
课程导入

British European Airways Flight 548
英国欧洲航空公司（BEA）548 航班

On an unseasonably cold and wet Sunday on June 18, 1972, 112 people boarded the British European Airways (BEA) flight 548 to Brussels from Heathrow Airport. It would never reach its destination. None of the 118 people on board survived.

1972 年 6 月 18 日，在一个异常寒冷潮湿的星期天，有 112 名乘客从希思罗机场登上了飞往布鲁塞尔的英国欧洲航空公司（BEA）548 航班。航班坠毁，机上 118 人无一生还。

Within 150 seconds of take off, disaster struck and the Trident 1 G-ARPI plummeted from the sky and crashed in a field in Staines, and burst into flames.

在起飞后的 150 秒，灾难发生了，三叉戟客机从空中坠落到斯泰恩斯地区，并起火燃烧。

The flight had been delayed by more than 20 minutes on that fateful Sunday from its scheduled take-off of 3:45pm, due to a readjustment of its load. Among the crew, who had been on standby, were 51-year-old Captain Stanley Key, 24-year-old Second Officer (SO) Simon Ticehurst and 22-year-old SO Jeremy Keighley.

该航班原定于下午 3 点 45 分起飞，但由于调整配载，飞机延误了 20 多分钟后才起飞。执行飞行任务的是 51 岁的机长斯坦利 · 基（Stanley Key）和 24 岁的副驾驶西蒙 · 泰斯赫斯特（Simon Ticehurst）和 22 岁的副驾驶杰里米 · 基斯利（Jeremy Keighley）。

In 1972, British European Airways was experiencing significant turmoil in the workplace. Many younger pilots wanted to organize a ***strike*** to demand higher wages and better working conditions, while older, traditional pilots generally opposed the action. The proposed strike exposed a generational divide between those who viewed flying as a passion versus those who viewed it as a career. Lively arguments became commonplace.

1972 年，英国欧洲航空公司（British European Airways）正经历着管理混乱。许多年轻的飞行员想要组织**罢工**，以期获得更高的薪水和更好的工作环境，而年长老派的飞行员则反对罢工这一举动。这次筹备中的罢工也暴露了挚爱飞行事业的飞行员和以飞行工作为谋生手段的飞行员之间的代沟。飞行队伍中充斥着激烈的争论。

The final report, published by High Court judge Sir Geoffrey Lane in 1973, found there was a "consistent failure by the handling pilot to achieve the appropriate speeds for the relevant stages of the flight".

英国高等法院法官杰弗里 · 莱恩爵士于 1973 年发表的最后一份报告指出，“操控飞机的飞行员未能让飞机达到飞行相关阶段的适当速度是造成空难的原因”。

The crew made their first fatal error after just 114 seconds when they retracted the aircraft's wing slats when doing speeds of 162 knots-60 knots below the required speed-causing the plane to stall.

当飞机以 162 节（比要求速度低 60 节）的速度飞行时，机组收起缝翼。机组人员在

114 秒后就犯了第一个致命错误，导致飞机失速。

Several ***stall warnings*** went unnoticed by the crew before the aircraft fell to a height where no recovery was possible.

飞机下坠到一个无法改出的高度前，**失速警告**并没有引起机组的注意。

More startling would be the investigation's conclusion that Captain Key's judgement had been impaired by a heart condition, which was likely to have been causing him some pain immediately prior to the crash. The investigation said a "violent argument" over strike action involving Captain Key and a first officer in the crew room an hour-and-a-half before departure. Stanley ' s communication with the tower appears to be extremely brief, which may be evidence of his indisposition.

更令人吃惊的是，调查得出的结论是，当时机长可能突发心脏病，感觉到心脏疼痛并影响判断力。调查表明，飞机起飞前一个半小时，机长曾与一名副驾驶在员工休息室就罢工一事发生了“激烈争执”。斯坦利与塔台间的通信内容也显得极为简短，也可能是其身体不适的旁证。

Investigators have also been able to piece together what happened to Flight 548. The strike led to the altercation that led to Captain Stanley's heart attack, and similardesigned levers made pilots prone to error, and the co-pilot was afraid to speak at critical moments. The superposition of all kinds of accidents finally penetrated the security line.

调查员也理出了 548 号航班事故的脉络，罢工事件导致斯坦利机长卷入了争吵冲突，继而引发了他的心脏病，外观相似的操作杆设计让飞行员非常容易出错，副驾驶在关键时刻也不敢发声。种种意外事件的叠加，最终击穿了安全防线。

Key words
关键词

strike	罢工
stall warnings	失速警告

Discussion
讨论

(1) How to create a good atmosphere in the cockpit?
(2) As the captain, how to lead the whole crew to complete the flight mission better?
(3) As a co-pilot, how to cooperate with the captain to complete the flight mission?
(1) 如何营造驾驶舱的良好氛围?
(2) 作为机长，如何领导整个机组更好地完成飞行任务?
(3) 作为副驾驶，如何配合机长完成飞行任务?

Advanced thinking
高阶思维

Collect information about British European Airways Filight 548, understand the causes of stall, and summarize the causes of stall in air crashes in recent 20 years.

收集关于英国欧洲航空公司（BEA）548 航班的资料，了解失速的原因，并总结近二十年来空难中出现失速的原因。

Table　Causes of stall in air accidents in recent 20 years

表　近二十年来空难中出现失速的原因

Air accident 空难	Time of occurrence 发生时间	Aircraft type 机型	Reason 原因

Lesson 12　Cockpit Managerial Grid and Leadership
第 12 课　驾驶舱管理网格和驾驶舱领导

12.1　Cockpit Managerial Grid
12.1　驾驶舱管理网格

The treatment of task orientation and people orientation as two independent dimensions was a major step in leadership studies. Many of the leadership studies conducted in the 1950s at the University of Michigan and the Ohio State University focused on these two dimensions.

领导力研究将任务取向和人的取向视为两个独立的维度。在 20 世纪 50 年代，密歇根大学和俄亥俄州立大学的许多关于领导力的研究都集中在这两个方面。

Building on the work of the researchers at these Universities, Robert Blake and Jane Mouton (1960s) proposed a graphic portrayal of leadership styles through a managerial grid (sometimes called leadership grid), as shown in Figure 12-1. The grid depicted two dimensions of leader behavior, concern for pople on y-axis and concern for production on x-axis, with each dimension ranging from low (1) to high (9), thus creating 81 different positions in which the leader's style may fall.

在这些大学研究人员工作的基础上，罗伯特·布莱克（Robert Blake）和简·莫顿（Jane Mouton）在 20 世纪 60 年代提出了一种通过管理网格（有时被称为领导网格）来描绘领导风格的观点，如图 12-1 所示。网格从两个维度描述了领导风格，分别是纵轴（对人的关心）、横轴（对绩效的关心），第 1 格表示关心程度最小，第 9 格表示关心程度最大。全图总共 81 个小方格，分别表示“对绩效的关心”和“对人的关心”这两个基本因素以不同比例结合的领导方式。

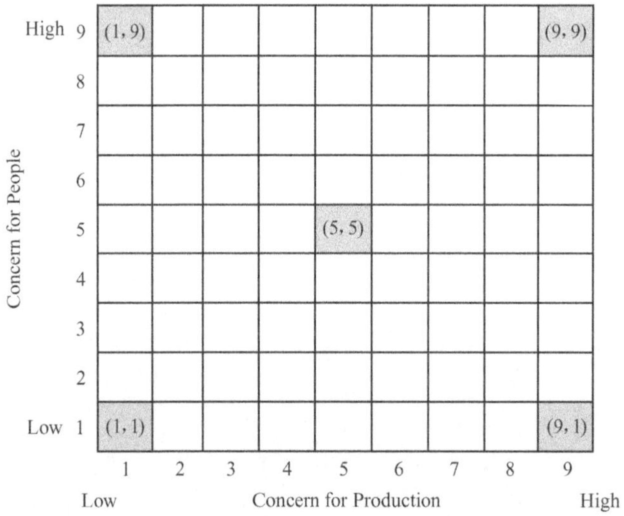

Figure 12-1　Managerial grid

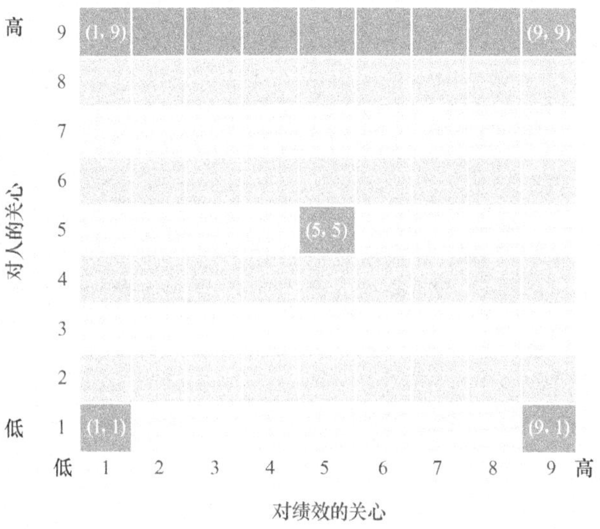

图 12-1　管理网格

扫一扫查看彩图

The five resulting leadership styles are as follows:

由此产生的五种领导风格如下:

(1) Impoverished Management (1, 1): Managers with this approach are low on both the dimensions and exercise minimum effort to get the work done from subordinates. The leader has low concern for employee satisfaction and work deadlines and as a result disharmony and disorganization prevail within the organization. The leaders are termed ineffective wherein their action is merely aimed at preserving job and seniority.

(1) 贫乏管理型 (1, 1): 使用这种方法的管理的领导者在这两个维度上都很低, 并且在指导下属的工作上花费的精力最少。领导者不太关心员工的满意度和工作期限, 组织内部普遍存在不和谐和无组织现象。这些领导者被称为无效领导, 因为他们的行动仅仅是为了保住自己的工作和资历。

(2) Task management (9, 1): Here leaders are more concerned about production and have less concern for people. The employees' needs are not taken care of and they are simply a means to an end. The leader believes that efficiency can result only through proper organization of work systems and through elimination of people wherever possible.

(2) 任务管理型 (9, 1): 这种领导者更关心工作业绩, 不太关心员工。员工的需求没有得到照顾, 领导者只是通过这种管理模式达到工作目的。领导者相信只有通过适当的企业组织和人员精简, 就能提高工作效率。

(3) Middle-of-the-Road (5, 5): This is basically a compromising style wherein the leader tries to maintain a balance between goals of company and the needs of people. Here neither employee nor production needs are fully met.

(3) 自我中心型 (5, 5): 这基本上是一种妥协风格, 领导者试图在绩效目标和员工需求之间保持平衡。实际上，员工和生产的需求都没有得到充分满足。

(4) Country Club (1, 9): This is characterized by low task and high people orientation where the leader gives thoughtful attention to the needs of people thus providing them with a friendly and comfortable environment. The leader feels that such a treatment with employees will lead to self-motivation and will find people working hard on their own. However, a low focus on tasks can hamper production and lead to questionable results.

(4) 乡村俱乐部型 (1, 9): 特点是任务量少，以人为本，领导者对人的需求给予全方位的关注，为员工提供一个友好和舒适的环境。领导者认为这种对待员工的方式会激发员工的自我激励，从而努力工作。但是，这种管理方式对工作业绩低关注，会影响工作质量，后患无穷。

(5) Team Management (9, 9): Characterized by high people and task focus, the style has been termed as most effective style according to Blake and Mouton. The leader feels that empowerment, commitment, trust, and respect are the key elements in creating a team atmosphere which will automatically result in high employee satisfaction and production.

(5) 团队管理型 (9, 9): 以高度关注人的需求和工作业绩为特点，被布莱克和莫顿认为是最有效的风格。领导者认为授权、承诺、信任和尊重是创造团队氛围的关键因素，这种氛围自然而然地使得员工的满意度提升、生产业绩提高。

The Managerial or Leadership Grid is used to help managers analyze their own leadership styles through a technique known as grid training. The training is aimed at basically helping leaders reach to the ideal state of (9, 9).

管理或领导网格是用来帮助管理者通过一种称为网格训练的技术来分析他们自己的领导风格。培训的主要目的是帮助领导者达到 (9, 9) 的理想状态。

12.2　What is the Differences Between Captain and Co-pilot?

12.2　机长和副驾驶的区别

Flight crews include a captain and at least one co-pilot. Pilots in both roles need to be capable of flying the aircraft and managing the flight. After all, if something happens to the captain, the co-pilot needs to take over. However, these roles are not exactly the same. The captain takes on more responsibility than his co-pilot, even though they share duties during the flight.

机组成员包括一名机长和至少一名副驾驶。这两种角色的飞行员都需要具备驾驶飞机和管理飞行的能力。毕竟，如果机长出现特殊情况，副驾驶就得接手操作管理飞机。然而，这两种角色并不完全相同。尽管他们在飞行过程中共同承担飞行任务和职责，机长比副驾驶承担更多的责任。

Duties of a Captain

机长的职责

The captain is responsible for the flight, the crew, the passengers and the aircraft. He has to ensure that all necessary checks are made before, during and after the flight. Typically, this role is responsible for weather checks, safety checklists, flight planning and flying the plane to its destination. Pilots also report any issues or changes during flights, take note of communications from air traffic control personnel and adapt flight plans if required.

机长要对飞行、机组人员、乘客和飞机负责。他必须确保在飞行前、飞行中和飞行后进行所有必要的检查。通常，机长负责天气检查、安全检查清单、飞行计划和驾驶飞机到达目的地机场。此外，报告飞行过程中的任何问题或变化，注意空中交通管制人员的通话，并根据需要调整飞行计划。

The captain does not necessarily delegate only routine tasks to his co-pilot. The two tend to share all tasks, including flying the plane. In emergencies, the captain may hand over all routine tasks to the co-pilot while he manages the situation.

机长不仅让副驾驶完成常规任务，也需要副驾驶可以分担包括驾驶飞机在内的所有任务。在紧急情况下，机长可以将所有常规工作移交给副驾驶，自己来处理紧急情况。

Duties of a Co-pilot

副驾驶的职责

There are no flight tasks that the co-pilot, or first officer, cannot or does not do, although the captain will direct the co-pilot's responsibilities for each flight. Typically, the two share flight tasks, though the co-pilot might be responsible for working the communication radios and navigational computers. On longer flights, a co-pilot might assume command when the captain takes a scheduled break, or they may switch responsibilities for flying and other tasks on each leg of the flight.

尽管机长会在每次飞行中给副驾驶指令，让副驾驶完成自己的职责，实际上，其他的飞行任务副驾驶也是可以操作的。通常情况下，这两名飞行员分担飞行任务，副驾驶负责无线电通信和导航的工作。在长途飞行中，副驾驶可能会在机长计划休息的时候接手管理飞行，也可能会在任何一段飞行中与机长转换职责。

The co-pilot will also take command if the captain becomes ill or incapacitated.

如果机长生病或失能，副驾驶也会履行机长职责。

Death in the air: American Airlines pilot dies mid-flight with 152 on board

空中死亡：美国航空公司飞行员在飞行途中死亡，机上有 152 人

The captain of an American Airlines flight died while piloting his plane, which was carrying 147 passengers and 5 crew members from Phoenix to Boston, the airline has confirmed. The cause of death is still unknown, except that it was due to an "illness."

美国航空公司证实，一架载有 147 名乘客和 5 名机组人员的飞机从凤凰城飞往波士顿，机长在驾驶飞机中死亡。死亡原因目前还不清楚，只知道是由于“疾病”。

"Syracuse, American 550, medical emergency, captain is incapacitated, request handling for runway," the co－pilot is heard saying on an audio recording posted on savvystews. com, which provides only a glimpse into the dramatic events that transpired in the plane's cockpit on Monday.

在网站上的一段录音中，可以听到副驾驶说：“锡拉丘兹，美国 550 航空公司，要求

紧急医疗，机长目前失能，请求优先着陆。”这段录音只是对周一发生在驾驶舱中的戏剧性事件的一个小缩影。

The Airbus A320's first officer was recorded talking to the control tower in Syracuse, New York, where Flight 550 requested an emergency landing.

这架空客 A320 的副驾驶与纽约锡拉丘兹塔台管制人员的通话被记录了下来，550 航班在锡拉丘兹请求紧急降落。

Lesson 13　Trans-cockpit Authority Gradient
第 13 课　驾驶舱职权梯度

Authority of the Commander and the Assertiveness of the Co-pilot
机长的权威性和副驾驶的直陈性

How many Captains are there on board? This is a tricky question, since the entire aircraft could theoretically be filled with Captains. However, there is only one Commander on board. As the Pilot In Command (PIC), the Captain has the ultimate responsibility and authority over the flight, but the co-pilot must have the ability to question the Captain when appropriate. This ability is called assertiveness.

飞机上有多少位机长？这个问题不太好回答，因为从理论上讲，整架飞机可以坐满了机长。然而，飞机上只有一名指挥官。作为机长（PIC），他/她对飞行有最终的责任和权力，但副驾驶必须具备在适当的时候质疑机长的能力，这种能力被称为副驾驶的直陈性。

The balance between the authority of the commander and the assertiveness of the co-pilot is called the trans-cockpit authority gradient. If the Captain acts like a dictator and the co-pilot is reserved, the gradient is steep. On the flipside, if the Captain needs to gain approval from every team member before making a decision, the gradient is close to zero. None of these scenarios are desirable. In the first example, teamwork will be close to non-existent - In the second example, communication and responsibilities may be blurred.

机长的权威性和副驾驶的直陈性之间的平衡被称为驾驶舱职权梯度。如果机长表现得像一个独裁者，而副驾驶不敢表达自己的观点，那么这个飞行机组的驾驶舱职权梯度就会过陡。另一方面，如果机长需要在做出决定前获得每个团队成员的同意，那么这个飞行机组的驾驶舱职权梯度就接近于零。这两种情况都不是理想的驾驶舱职权梯度。在第一个例子中，团队合作将几乎不存在。在第二个例子中，沟通和责任可能会模糊。

A middle ground in between these two examples gives us a favorable work climate, or what we would call good Crew Resource Management (CRM).

以上这两种驾驶舱职权梯度之间就是一个良好的工作环境，我们可以称之为好的机组资源管理（CRM）。

Please consider about the questions as below.

请考虑以下问题。

(1) Which is the more valued role, a leader or a team player?

(2) Do you like working with others?

(3) What makes the perfect team?

(4) Give an example of when you demonstrated good leadership?

(5) Do you consider Cabin Crew to be as important as Pilots in a team?

(6) As a leader, you have to make a difficult decision on behalf of the team, would you seek advice from others?

(7) Describe what your leadership style is like, is it the best, is it always the same for every situation?

(1) 团队领导和队员，哪个角色更重要？

(2) 你是否喜欢与别人一起工作？

(3) 什么样的团队是完美团队？

(4) 举例你曾表现卓越领导力的一件事。

(5) 你是否认为乘务组和飞行员一样重要？

(6) 作为团队领导，如果你需要代表整个团队做决策，你是否会咨询其他成员的建议？

(7) 描述一下你的领导风格是怎样的。是不是最优化的？在不同情境下，你的领导风格是否保持一致？

Flight Training Files
飞行训练档案

Case
案例

Xiao Ming's first instructor resigned from the flight school for personal reasons. It's heard that the new instructor was a very old man. He had served in the Air Force before, and returned back to teaching at the flight school after retiring from the airliner company because he had interest in teaching. The first time he met Xiao Ming was not nice, the old man said that Xiao Ming had better forget all the things taught by the previous instructor. Xiao Ming was an introverted person, so he dared not speak. The new instructor has been talking about how he used to be in the army and aviation company in their first flight, finally he approached the wrong runway, because he was not familiar with the training airport. Xiao Ming noticed the problem as he approached, but he did not dare to suggest it to the instructor. He felt that a senior instructor would not make such a silly mistake.

小明的首任教员因为个人原因从航校离职了。听说新的教员是个年纪挺大的人，以前在空军服役过，在航空公司干到退休后又因兴趣回到了航校教书。第一次见面小明就被这位新教员一顿数落，新教员表示他来了，那么以前教员教的东西全部都作废了，要按他教的来。小明本就是比较内向的人，被教员这么一说就不敢说话了。新教员在第一班飞行中一直在说以前自己在部队和航司如何，但由于对航校训练机场不熟悉，最后进近落错了跑道。小明在进近时就发现了问题，但他不敢向教员提出，他觉得资历如此丰富的老教员不会犯这种错误。

Briefing
讲评

No matter as a cadet now or a captain in the future, you should take care of the cockpit gradient, not make communicating too hard. The instructor in the example might be an expert in flying. But his experience in the training airport is limited. When you get confused during the flight, talk to your partner or instructor.

无论是作为学员还是将来成为机长，都要注意控制驾驶舱梯度，不要让驾驶舱中的交流变得太困难。例子中的新教员虽然飞行经历可能很丰富，但他在航校机场的运行时间可能很短，在飞行中有疑惑时要及时提出，与搭档/教员讨论。

Unit 6
Cockpit Automation

第 6 篇　驾驶舱自动化

Lead-in
课程导入

Everything you need to know about the Boeing 737 Max airplane crashes
关于波音 737 Max 飞机坠毁你需要知道的一切

The crashes of Lion Air Flight 610 and Ethiopian Airlines Flight 302 have rocked the aviation industry, sparked numerous investigations, and resulted in the grounding of hundreds of Boeing 737 Max jets worldwide.

狮航 610 号航班和埃塞俄比亚航空 302 号航班的坠毁震惊了航空业，从而引发了大量调查，并导致全球数百架波音 737 Max 飞机停飞。

What happened?

发生了什么事?

Lion Air Flight 610 took off from Jakarta, Indonesia on Monday, October 29th, 2018, at 6: 20am local time. Its destination was Pangkal Pinang, the largest city of Indonesia's Bangka Belitung Islands. Twelve minutes after takeoff, the plane crashed into the Java Sea, killing all 189 passengers and crew.

当地时间 2018 年 10 月 29 日（周一）早上 6 点 20 分，狮航 610 航班从印尼雅加达起飞。它的目的地是印尼邦加勿里洞群岛（Bangka Belitung Islands）最大的城市邦加尔槟城（Pangkal Pinang）。飞机起飞 12 分钟后坠入爪哇海，机上 189 名乘客和机组人员全部遇难。

Nearly five months later, Ethiopian Airlines Flight 302 took off from Addis Ababa, Ethiopia on Sunday, March 10th, 2019, at 8: 38am local time. Its destination was Nairobi, Kenya. Six minutes after takeoff, the plane crashed near the town of Bishoftu, Ethiopia, killing all 157 people aboard.

5 个月后，埃塞俄比亚航空 302 航班于当地时间 2019 年 3 月 10 日上午 8 点 38 分从埃塞俄比亚首都亚的斯亚贝巴起飞。它的目的地是肯尼亚内罗毕。飞机起飞 6 分钟后在埃塞俄比亚的比斯霍夫图附近坠毁，机上 157 人全部遇难。

Both crashed jets were Boeing 737 Max 8s, a variant of the best-selling aircraft in history. When Airbus announced in 2010 it would make a new fuel-efficient and cost-effective plane, Boeing rushed to get out its own version. That version was the 737 Max airplanes.

两架坠毁的飞机都是波音 737 Max 8，是历史上最畅销飞机波音 737 装配新发动机的衍生机型。当空客在 2010 年宣布它将生产一款节油低成本的新机型时，波音也急着推出自己的新机型。那款新机型就是 737 Max。

What caused these crashes?

是什么导致了这些事故?

A preliminary report from Indonesian investigators indicates that Lion Air 610 crashed because a faulty sensor erroneously reported that the airplane was ***stalling***. The false report triggered an automated system known as the Maneuvering Characteristics Augmentation System, or

MCAS. This system tried to point the aircraft's nose down so that it could gain enough speed to fly safely.

印尼调查人员的初步报告显示，狮航610航班坠毁的原因是一个有故障的传感器错误地报告飞机失速。这一虚假报告触发了一个被称为机动特征增强系统（MCAS）的自动化系统。这个系统试图将飞机的机头朝下，这样它就可以获得足够的速度来安全飞行。

What is MCAS?

什么是机动特征增强系统（MCAS）?

Boeing says the decision to include this change to the flight control operations wasn't arbitrary. When the company designed the Max jets, it made the engines larger to increase ***fuel efficiency***, and positioned them slightly forward and higher up on the plane's wings.

波音公司表示，将机动特征增强系统（MCAS）纳入飞行控制操作的决定并不是武断的。该公司在设计Max喷气式飞机时，为了提高燃油效率，将发动机做得更大，并将其放置在机翼上略微向前和更高的位置。

These tweaks changed how the jet handled in certain situations. The relocated engines caused the jet's nose to pitch skyward. To compensate, Boeing added a computerized system called MCAS to prevent the plane's nose from getting too high and causing a stall. MCAS is unique to the Max jets, and isn't present in other Boeing 737s.

这些调整改变了飞机在某些情况下的处理方式。引擎位置的上移导致飞机的机头向上倾斜。于是，波音公司增加了一个名为MCAS的计算机系统，以防止飞机的机头过高而导致失速。MCAS是Max飞机独有的，在其他波音737中没有出现。

About 30 airlines operated the Max by the time of the second crash (the three largest customers being Southwest Airlines, American Airlines and Air Canada). Most of them quickly grounded their planes a few days later. Besides the airlines already mentioned that list includes United Airlines, WestJet, Aeromexico, Aerolíneas Argentinas, GOL Linhas Aéreas, Turkish Airlines, FlyDubai, Air China, Copa Airlines, Norwegian, Hainan Airlines, Fiji Airways and Royal Air Maroc.

第二次坠机时，大约有30家航空公司在运营Max（最大的三个客户是西南航空、美国航空和加拿大航空）。几天后，大多数公司迅速将飞机停飞。除了已经提到的航空公司之外，停飞名单上还包括联合航空、西捷航空、墨西哥航空、阿根廷航空、高尔航空、土耳其航空、迪拜飞航、中国国航、巴拿马航空、挪威航空、海南航空、斐济航空和摩洛哥皇家航空。

Key words

关键词

MCAS (Maneuvering Characteristics Augmentation System)	机动特征增强系统
stall	失速
fuel efficiency	节油

Discussion
讨论

(1) Why MCAS is designed to be automatic control but not manual control?
(1) 为什么 MCAS 被设计成自动控制而不是手动控制?
(2) Do you consider that the automation has no disadvantage?
(2) 你是否认为自动化是没有缺点的?

Advanced thinking
高阶思维

What the Boeing company, the airlines and the pilots need to do to prepare if the 737 Max production is planned to be restarted?

如果波音 737 Max 项目被重启，波音公司、航空公司和飞行员应该做好哪些准备?

Boeing company 波音公司	Airlines 航空公司	Pilots 飞行员

Lesson 14　Human Factors and Cockpit Automation
第14课　驾驶舱自动化与人的因素

14.1　What is the Cockpit Automation
14.1　什么是驾驶舱自动化

Cockpit instruments are the main source of pilot information, and the cockpit is the workplace where pilots operate the aircraft. With the rapid development of aviation industry, cockpits are constantly changing. The new cockpit designs highlight the human factor better, so that pilots can operate the aircraft in an easier, more comfortable and safer way. Look at the two different cockpits shown in Figure 14-1 and Figure 14-2 as below, find out the differences, and discuss which cockpit take the human element into considerations better.

驾驶舱仪表是飞行员获得信息的主要来源，驾驶舱是飞行员操作飞机的工作场所。航空事业飞速发展，驾驶舱也在不断变化，新的驾驶舱设计中更好地突出了人的因素，因此，飞行员能够以更容易、更舒适和更安全的方式操纵飞机。请观察图14-1和图14-2中两个不同的驾驶舱，找出他们的区别，并讨论哪一种驾驶舱更好地体现了人的因素。

Figure 14-1　Cessna 172 cockpit
图14-1　塞斯纳172驾驶舱

扫一扫查看彩图

Figure 14-2　Boeing 737 cockpit
图 14-2　波音 737 驾驶舱

扫一扫查看彩图

Boeing 737 cockpit design characterized by computer generated visual displays, at least a Primary Flight Display (PFD) and a Navigation Display (ND) connected to a Flight Management System (FMS) which is called Glass Cockpit.

波音 737 驾驶舱设计的特点是基于计算机技术的显示器，有与飞行管理系统（FMS）相连的主飞行显示（PFD）和一个导航显示（ND），这种驾驶舱被叫作玻璃驾驶舱。

As shown in Figure 14-3, In front of the pilot and co-pilot in the cockpit of the C919, there are five large screens showing flight status, navigation information, alarm information, schematic pages and so on. When the aircraft is in different phases, the pilot needs to pay attention to different information, such as the taxi phase, the pilot needs to pay attention to the tire temperature and tire pressure of the landing gear, but during the cruise phase, this information is no longer the focus of the pilot. Therefore, in the design of theinstrument display system of C919, the designers have fully sorted out and classified the display information. Through logical programming, the information that pilots do not need to pay attention to during taxiing, takeoff, climbing, cruising, descending and landing of the aircraft is inhibited and the information that needs to be paid attention to is sorted. In this way, the screen will only display the pilot need to pay attention to information, through this information, the pilot can immediately understand the status of the aircraft, no longer needs to manually obtain information, also does not need to filter the needed information, reduces the workload. It can also avoid mis-operation caused by human factors. At the same time, the C919 has backed up 30 options for reconstructing the display area in case of screen failure. For example, if one screen suddenly fails, key information will be immediately reconstructed and displayed on other screens.

如图 14-3 所示，在 C919 驾驶舱正副驾驶员的前面，有 5 块大屏幕显示器，分别显示飞行状态、导航信息、告警信息、简图页等。当飞机处于不同阶段时，飞行员需要关注的

Figure 14-3　C919 cockpit
图 14-3　C919 驾驶舱

扫一扫查看彩图

信息各有不同，比如滑行阶段，飞行员需要关注起落架的胎温、胎压，而在巡航阶段，这些信息不再是飞行员关注的重点。因此，在 C919 飞机驾驶舱显示系统设计中，设计人员充分对显示信息进行了梳理分类，通过逻辑编程，将飞机在滑行、起飞、爬升、巡航、下降、着陆等各个阶段飞行员不需要关注的信息进行抑制，需要关注的信息进行排序。这样一来，屏幕上只会显示飞行员需要关注的信息，通过这些信息，飞行员可以第一时间了解飞机的状态，不再需要手动调取信息，也不需要筛选最需要的信息，既减轻了飞行员的工作负荷，也避免了人为因素引起的误操作。同时，C919 飞机还备份了 30 种屏幕失效情况下重新构建显示区域的方案，例如，如果其中有一块屏幕忽然失效了，关键信息会立即进行重构，显示在其他屏幕上。

An automated aircraft is generally comprised of an integrated advanced avionics system consisting of a primary flight display (PFD), a multifunction flight display (MFD) and a fully integrated autopilot. This type of aircraft is commonly known as an advanced avionics aircraft.

自动化飞机通常由一个集成的先进航空电子系统组成，包括一个主飞行显示器（PFD）、一个多功能飞行显示器（MFD）以及自动驾驶。这种类型的飞机通常被认为是配备了先进航电技术。

Automation is the single most important advance in aviation technologies. Electronic flight displays (EFDs) have made vast improvements in how information is displayed and what information is available to the pilot. Pilots can access electronic databases that contain all of the information traditionally contained in multiple handbooks, reducing clutter in the flight deck. Multifunction displays (MFDs) are capable of displaying moving maps that mirror sectional charts. MFDs are so descriptive that many pilots fall into the trap of relying solely on the moving maps for navigation. Pilots also draw upon the database to familiarize themselves with departure and destination airport information.

自动化是航空技术中最重要的一项进步。电子飞行显示器（EFDs）在信息显示方式和飞行员可获得的信息方面取得了巨大的进步。飞行员可以访问电子数据库，其中包含了传统上包含在多本手册中的所有信息，从而减少了驾驶舱里的混乱。多功能显示器（MFDs）能够显示移动地图。多功能显示器（MFDs）具有描述性，以至于许多飞行员陷入了过度依赖移动地图导航的陷阱。飞行员也利用这个数据库来熟悉始发地和目的地机场信息。

There are concerns about the effect of automation on pilots. In a study published in 1995, the British Airline Pilots Association officially voiced its concern that "Airline pilots increasingly lack 'basic flying skills' as a result of reliance on automation." This reliance on automation translates into a lack of basic flying skills that may affect the pilot's ability to cope with an inflight emergency, such as sudden mechanical failure. The worry that pilots are becoming too reliant on automated systems and are not being encouraged or trained to fly manually has grown with the increase in the number of MFD flight decks.

有人担心自动化对飞行员的影响。在 1995 年发表的一项研究中，英国航空公司飞行员协会（British Airline Pilots Association）正式表达了它的担忧，即“由于对自动化的依赖，航空公司飞行员越来越缺乏‘基本的飞行技能’。”这种对自动化的依赖意味着飞行员缺乏基本的飞行技能，这可能会影响飞行员应对飞行紧急情况（比如突然发生机械故障）的能力。随着日益提高的多功能数字座舱的数量，人们越来越担心飞行员正变得过于依赖自动系统，不鼓励飞行员使用自动驾驶，或是训练飞行员手动飞行。

In summary, cockpit automation:

(1) Apply computer display technology.

(2) Pilots can compile and manage flight procedures through a powerful aircraft management system.

(3) Instead of mechanical connections, software and wires introduce high intelligence into the operating system, providing the operator with unprecedented modes of operation and protection.

综上，驾驶舱自动化：

(1) 计算机显示技术的使用。

(2) 通过功能强大的飞机管理系统，飞行员可以编辑、管理飞行的程序。

(3) 软件和电线代替了机械连接，将高智能引入操作系统，向操作人员提供前所未有的操作模式和保护。

14.2 Some Basic Definitions
14.2 基本概念

Some ambiguities and arguments about automation result from the absence of unified vocabulary. The notion of automation itself covers a wide variety of systems featuring verify different modes of interaction with the crew. This section therefore provides definitions for a number of concepts related to cockpit automation.

自动化本身包含了许多系统，不同的自动化系统的人机交流模式也不尽相同。下面我们将简单介绍一下不同的自动化系统和其他基本概念。

Automation

System or part of a system performing a predetermined action (or sequence of actions), with complete autonomy, when activated. Under standard conditions, pilots have no control over automations. Automations are mainly embedded in the execution chain of a given function, and are not directly visible to the pilots.

自动化

自动化是指在启动后，以完全自动的方式使整个或部分系统执行预定的行为（或按顺序行为）。在通常条件下，飞行员无须控制自动化系统。自动化主要用于一定功能的执行链中，飞行员无法直接看到。

Protection Automations

They are triggered when a safety limit is exceeded, the pilot cannot disengage them.

自动保护

超过设计的安全极限时，自动保护功能被启动；飞行员无法断开它们。

Automated System

Functional unit generally composed of automations. Under standard conditions, its activation results from a deliberate decision made by the pilots. It can be disengaged at any moment. Automated systems execute parts of high-level tasks that could also be performed by the pilot in manual mode. This is the use for the autopilot in its different modes, the auto-thrust, the auto-break, etc. modern, computerized automated systems are more accurate and offer a number of sophisticated modes, and process far more parameters than previous systems.

自动化系统

功能组件通常是由自动装置组成，在一般情况下，飞行员主动地启动自动装置，自动装置随时可以脱开。自动系统执行部分高级任务，飞行员也可以进行人工操作。例如，自动驾驶仪处于不同的工作方式、自动油门、自动刹车等。现代计算机自动系统更加准确，并提供了许多复杂工作方式，比以前的系统处理的参数要多。

Aid System

System displaying computer generated synthetic information. Automated diagnostic or troubleshooting systems displaying clear information on ECAMS (Airbus) or EICAS (Boeing) screes, Flight Directors (FD) meet this definition.

辅助系统

辅助系统显示计算机生成信息。将信息清楚地显示在 ECAM（空客）和 EICAS（波音）的自动诊断和排故系统，飞行指引仪（FD）都是此类系统。

Automated Aircraft

Aircraft equipped with a sophisticated autopilot and a number of automated systems thereby allowing a two-crewmember complement.

自动化飞机

飞机上装有复杂的自动驾驶仪和许多自动系统，用于双人制机组。

Glass Cockpit

Cockpit design characterized by computer generated visual displays, at least a Primary Flight Display (PFD) and a Navigation Display (ND) connected to a Flight Management System (FMS).

玻璃驾驶舱

驾驶舱仪表设计的特征是计算机组成的显示器，有与飞行管理系统（FMS）相连的一个主飞行显示器（PFD）和导航显示器（ND）。

Fly by Wire Aircraft

Last generation of glass cockpit aircraft featuring fight controls controlled through computers and electrical signals, a high degree of computerized controls on all aircraft systems.

电传飞行

新式的玻璃驾驶舱飞机的特征是通过计算机和电信号控制飞机，高度自动化地控制飞机所有系统。

Lesson 15 Cockpit Automation and Flight Safety
第15课 驾驶舱自动化与飞行安全

15.1 The Positive Effects of Automation
15.1 自动化的优点

Cockpit automation has many advantages, which can be summarized in the following aspects: First, it can complete many continuous tasks, reduce the workload of the pilot, so that the pilot can have more energy to complete more important tasks, such as decision-making. Second, due to the automation of the cockpit, many people's sources of error can be removed. If human operation can be replaced by stable and reliable machines, then human's changeability and fallibility can be overcome. Third, it can reduce cockpit space and provide better fuel management, all of which helps reduce the cost of flying. Fourth, cockpit automation can provide smoother and more precise control than manual operation. Fifth, realize computer control and program display.

驾驶舱自动化具有许多优点，概括起来主要有以下几方面：第一，它能够完成许多持续性的任务，减轻飞行员的工作负荷，使飞行员能够有更多的精力去完成更为重要的任务，如决策。第二，由于驾驶舱的自动化，可以去掉许多来源于人的错误。如果能够用性能稳定、可靠的机器去代替人类操作的话，那么人类的易变性和易犯错误的状态就可以得到克服。第三，能够减小驾驶舱空间，提供更好的燃油管理，所有这些都有助于降低飞行成本。第四，驾驶舱自动化能够比人工操作具有更为平稳、精确地控制。第五，实现计算机控制和程序显示。

15.2 The Drawbacks of Automation
15.2 自动化的缺点

15.2.1 Transformation of the Pilot's Role with Automation
15.2.1 使用自动化设备后的飞行员职责的转变

Design originally hoped to reduce the workload and difficulty of carrying our certain phases of the flight. It relieves pilots from repetitive sequences which were unrewarding and for which human performance is not consistent. It reinforces the gratifying part of pilots' jobs: decision making. However, these objectives have not always been reached and at times the outcomes have been diametrically opposed to these original goals. It seems in fact that certain fundamental principles in hum factors have all too often been forgotten.

自动化设计的初衷是减轻飞行员的工作负荷和难度，使飞行员不再做重复劳动，并帮助飞行员进行决策的制订。然而，实际的结果往往与设计目标完全相反。这是由于这些设计无法兼顾所有的人的因素方面的问题。

The human brain needs a certain degree of stimulation to remain alert. The situational awareness updating is driven by the cation plan, and its related intentions and expectations. A minimal workload is thus the prerequisite for good cognitive performance. Below this minimum level, the brain is in a standby state. Human operators are consequently poor supervisors of automated system, particularly when the system is very reliable and when few events are visible, such as cruise phase. If emergency issue happens, our brain can not reflect the situation timely resulting in the increase of workload till to the maximum.

人脑需要一定的刺激才能保持警惕；在行动计划、相关预期的条件下人们的情景意识会改变；最低工作负荷是保持良好的认知状态的先决条件，低于这个标准大脑会处于“休息”状态。在自动化状态下，飞行员要监视自动化系统的运行状态。尤其是在巡航阶段，自动化系统可靠性高，飞行员任务量少的情况下，如果遇到突发情况，大脑在这种休息状态下很难及时做出反应，导致工作负荷陡增至峰值。

15. 2. 2　Bias in Decision Making

15. 2. 2　决策偏见

EFIS, particularly the map display, has considerably facilitated navigation while automated diagnostic and advisory systems such as ECAM on Airbus aircraft and EICAS on Boeing aircraft, paly a major role in supporting pilots in dealing with aircraft systems. Consequently, EFIS and ECAM are considered by most pilots to strongly support situation awareness and decision making.

电子飞行仪表系统的独特之处在于其地图显示为导航提供便利，空客的 ECAM 和波音的 EICAS 等自动分析和咨询系统在辅助飞行员进行信息处理方面起到重要作用，这样一来，大多数飞行员认为 ECAM 或 EICAS 能帮助飞行员提高情景意识，辅助决策。

In fact, automation devices fools the pilot sometimes. If there is a lack of understanding or kinds of misunderstanding of automation devices, pilots will fall into the decision trap.

但事实上，这些自动设备常常会愚弄飞行员。如果对这类设备认识不足或者理解有误，就会陷入决策陷阱。

15. 2. 3　Complacency or Over-reliance on Automation

15. 2. 3　自满或过分依赖自动化设备

Complacency in the cockpit means that the pilot feels bored, has low alertness, lacks of attention and even lacks of the motivation to follow procedures and standards. Automated equipment makes pilots increasingly dependent on it to complete their flights. Pilots have confidence in the automated equipment and feel comfortable with it. The former active monitoring has become passive monitoring. They only need to confirm the display and look around from time to time, but lack of vigilance.

驾驶舱内的自满情绪意味着：飞行员感到乏味，低警觉性，缺乏注意甚至缺乏按照程序和标准规范操作的动机。自动化设备使飞行员逐步地依赖它来完成飞行。飞行员对自动化设备很有信心，感觉到自动化设备参与的飞行过程很舒适，以前的主动监控已经成为被动监控，飞行员只需要确认显示内容，不时张望一下，导致警惕性下降。

Monitoring a system that runs almost perfectly on its own is a boring task, while failing to monitor it can threaten safety. This risk of missing a mode change or mode reversion, of misunderstanding the actual behavior of automation or of not detecting an abnormal auto-flight performance is increased.

监视一个正常运行的系统是一件非常无聊的工作，但如果没有监控，它可能会威胁到飞机的安全。诸如飞行模式的修改、遗漏、反向选择或错误的理解系统，飞行员如果没有及时发现，它们将会直接威胁飞行安全。

15. 2. 4 Difficulties in Programming Automated Systems
15. 2. 4 自动化设备的编程困难

The revolution in flight management is due to the Flight Management System (FMS), which allows pilots to program a flight path from departure to destination, both for lateral and vertical navigation, and to couple this programmed flight plan to the autopilot for execution. The execution is then based on the automated management of feed back form the real world and on the reference to a model of the world stored in a database. The disadvantages are as follows:

自动管理的改进在于飞行管理系统（FMS）的出现，它便于飞行员在飞行前编订从起飞到目的地的水平导航和垂直导航的飞行程序，将飞行计划输入，交给自动驾驶去执行。自动驾驶执行程序根据实际外界反馈进行自动管理并参照储存在数据库中的模式进行工作。这种方式有消极作用：

(1) The consequences of errors have been shifted into the future: programming is lengthy and is often carried out under time pressure on stopovers. Without attentive checking, these errors remain in the black box and can cause abnormal flight behavior.

(1) 输入错误会影响后续飞行。编程是一个较长的过程，通常是在中转时间紧迫的情况下进行的，输入时的错误没有被检查出来，将会导致非预期的飞行动作。

(2) The use of databases is often a source of confusion for pilots with similar names, or incidents related to point coordinate errors within the database itself.

(2) 导航数据库的数据更新不及时也会导致飞行异常。数据库中相似的地名，也经常对飞行员造成迷惑。

American Airlines Flight 965

美联航 965 号班机

American Airlines Flight 965, a Boeing 757 was a scheduled flight from Miami International Airport in Miami, Florida, United States to Alfonso Bonilla Aragón International Airport in Cali, Colombia, which crashed into a mountain in Buga, Colombia on December 20, 1995, killing 151 passengers and 8 crew members.

美国航空 965 号班机（AA965）是美国航空一班从美国迈阿密前往哥伦比亚考卡山谷

省首府卡利的定期航班。1995 年 12 月 20 日，执飞此航班的一架波音 757 客机在考卡山谷省布加附近撞山坠毁，机上 151 名乘客，8 名机组人员遇难。

The aircraft was 63nm out of Cali VOR (which is 8nm South of the airport) at the time. Cali cleared the flight for a direct Cali VOR approach and report at Tulua VOR. Followed one minute later by a clearance for a straight in VOR DME approach to runway 19 (the Rozo 1 arrival).

飞机当时位于距卡利（Cali）的 VOR 台 63 海里（机场以南 8 海里）处。卡利允许该航班 VOR 直接进场，并在图卢瓦（Tulua）VOR 台报告。1 分钟后，飞机允许直线 VOR DME 进场 19 跑道。

The crew then tried to select the Rozo NDB (Non Directional Beacon) on the Flight Management Computer (FMC). Because their Jeppesen approach plates showed 'R'as the code for Rozo, the crew selected this option. But 'R'in the FMC database meant Romeo. Romeo is a navaid 150nm from Rozo, but has the same frequency. The aircraft had just passed Tulua VOR when it started a turn to the left (towards Romeo). This turn caused some confusion in the cockpit since Rozo 1 was to be a straight in approach. 87 seconds after commencing the turn, the crew activated Heading Select (HDG SEL), which disengaged LNAV and started a right turn. The left turn brought the B757 over mountainous terrain, so a Ground Proximity (GPWS) warning sounded. With increased engine power and nose-up the crew tried to climb. The spoilers were still activated however. The stick shaker then activated and the aircraft crashed into a mountain at about 8900 feet (Cali field elevation being 3153 feet).

机组人员随后试图在飞行管理计算机（FMC）上选择 Rozo NDB（无方向信标台）。在吉普逊进近图中，“R”是“Rozo”的代码，机组人员选择了这个选项。但在 FMC 数据库中，“R”对应的是“Romeo”。而“Romeo”距离“Rozo”150 海里，频率相同。飞机刚经过 Tulua VOR 台，就开始向左转弯（朝着 Romeo 方向）。这个转弯在驾驶舱内引起了一些混乱，因为 Rozo 1 是直线进近。开始转弯 87 秒后，乘员激活航向选择（HDG SEL），脱离水平导航并开始右转。但是前面的左转已经使飞机飞过山脉，因此近地告警系统（GPWS）响起。随着发动机功率增加和机头上仰，机组人员设法使飞机爬升。扰流板依旧处于放出位。然后，抖杆器开始抖振，飞机撞山，撞击点高度为 8900 英尺。

Possible causes are as follows:

可能的原因如下：

1) The flight crew's failure to adequately plan and execute the approach to runway 19 at SKCL and their inadequate use of automation.

1) 在向 19 跑道进近时，机组人员缺乏充分的计划，并对自动驾驶仪的使用不当。

2) Failure of the flight crew to discontinue the approach into Cali, despite numerous cues alerting them of the inadvisability of continuing the approach.

2) 尽管当时驾驶舱中多次出现告警提示他们连续进近不可取，他们仍然进行了不成功的连续进场。

3) The lack of situational awareness of the flight crew regarding vertical navigation, proximity to terrain, and the relative location of critical radio aids.

3) 机组人员缺乏对垂直导航、近地告警和紧急无线电设备的了解和警觉。

4) Failure of the flight crew to revert to basic radio navigation at the time when the FMS-assisted navigation became confusing and demanded an excessive workload in a critical phase of the flight.

4) 当 FMS 辅助导航系统发生混乱时，机组人员没有及时返回基础无线电导航系统，增加了关键飞行阶段的额外工作负荷。

5) The flight crew's ongoing efforts to expedite their approach and landing in order to avoid potential delays.

5) 飞行机组试图加速进场和着陆，以避免潜在的延误。

6) The flight crew's execution of the GPWS escape manoeuvre while the speed brakes remained deployed.

6) 飞行员在执行 GPWS 改出机动时，减速板仍在放出位置。

7) FMS logic that dropped all intermediate fixes from the display (s) in the event of execution of a direct routing.

7) 在执行直飞过程中，FMS 逻辑混乱，将之前所输入的中间的航路点全部删除了。

8) FMS-generated navigational information that used a different naming convention from that published in navigational charts.

8) FMS 生成的导航信息使用的名称与导航图中的信息不一致。

(3) In case of major changes in the flight plan, this implies a reprogramming of the FMS, which can take some time. There have been several reported incidents where pilots, after a go-around or a runway change on final approach, failed to get the new procedure on the screen and persisted for a fairly long time. Generally speaking, when the pilots with experience program the flight plan, they often leave some flexibility. Information about the go around procedure or another possible landing runway is taped in the backup procedure, alternate airport information is programmed in bad weather, etc. , and the backup procedure is only activated when the flight plan changes.

(3) 飞行计划要做较大修改时意味着需要重新更改飞行管理系统的程序，而更改需要消耗一定的时间，当复飞后或五边进近更换预定跑道时，飞行员如果重新编辑飞行程序就会给飞行带来压力。通常，有经验的飞行员在编制飞行计划时，会留有一定的裕度，在备用程序中输入复飞程序或另一条可能的着陆跑道的信息，在天气不好的时候输入备降场信息等，在飞行计划发生变化时只需要激活备用程序即可。

15.2.5 Difficulties in Crew Communication and Coordination

15.2.5 自动化导致的机组交流和配合困难

Glass cockpit architecture and technology provides an enhanced representation of the outside world, but it reduces the opportunities for non-verbal communication and synchronization between the two crew members. On average, fewer movements are required to do the tasks. Information is concentrated on fewer instruments, and controls are rationalist and concentrated on small surfaces. Some of the control gestures are impossible to decode form the crew partner's position. Even the motion of the flight and engine control systems-stick and throttles-is sometimes reduced.

Peripheral vision is thus losing prat of its efficiency. Also, tactile piloting-noise level and changes in attitude- is smoothed out by the computer. The glass cockpit design requires pilots to pay more attention to crew coordination to compensate for the loss of non-verbal communication.

玻璃驾驶舱的结构和技术增加了外界环境的参数显示，但减少了机组人员之间的非语言交流与行为的同步性。通常，完成一项任务所需的动作很少，信息显示在为数不多的几块仪表上，另一名机组人员不可能从手势上判断该飞行员在进行什么操作，机长无法猜出副驾驶在多功能显示器上输入了什么，甚至连操纵杆和油门杆的移动也减少了，使用眼角余光的作用也没有被充分使用。计算机也消除了靠触觉感受噪声大小和感知飞行姿态改变的可能性。因此，玻璃驾驶舱的设计需要飞行员更加注重机组的配合，以补偿非语言交流的损失。

15.2.6 Information Processing Difficulties
15.2.6 信息处理困难

The information in the cockpit tend to use written version to be displayed. The information is in English and is abbreviated. For the pilots whose mother tongue are not English, which takes a great number of time to read. The number of acronyms is so high that the less frequent ones tend to be ignored or confused with more frequent ones.

玻璃驾驶舱中的很多信息以书面形式显示处理。并且这些信息都用英语显示，且夹杂着大量的缩略语。对于以非英语为母语的国家的飞行员来说，阅读信息需要消耗大量时间。飞行员常常忽略出现频率不高的缩略语，或与常用的缩略语混淆。

15.3 How to Adapt Automation?
15.3 如何适应自动化?

15.3.1 Understanding Automation Philosophy
15.3.1 理解自动化理念

The first way to overcome automation drawbacks is to properly understand the philosophy behind automaton. Automation must be thought as a resource at the disposal of the crew, who are responsible for the safety of the flight, passenger comfort and efficiency. The crew has and must keep control, under the authority of the captain.

克服自动化缺陷的第一个方法是正确理解自动化理念。自动化是可供机组人员支配的资源，确保飞行的安全、乘客的舒适和飞行效率的应该是机组人员。机长需具有权威性，机组需保证控制飞机。

15.3.2 Adhering to Airline Automation Policy
15.3.2 遵守航空公司的自动化政策

It is aimed at answering questions such as: "What are good and usable guidelines for the operation of automation on the line? How do we influence the procurement of new additional equipment, such as Head-Up-Displays for automated flight decks?"

自动化政策旨在回答以下问题:“哪些是更好使用自动化的指南?平视显示器作为新的自动化设备应该如何使用?”

Here are some tips for you:

(1) Use of checklist, standard terminology and language in the cockpit.

(2) Call outs in use of the automatic flight system.

(3) Automation philosophy.

(4) Definition of levels of automation.

(5) Crew co-ordination, and task and role allocation between PF and PNF for each automation level.

以下是给你的一些建议:

(1) 在驾驶舱应使用检查单、标准术语和语言。

(2) 使用自动飞行时进行标准喊话。

(3) 理解自动化理念。

(4) 定义不同级别的自动化。

(5) 设置不同自动化级别下人员的协调方式,即机长和副驾驶之间的任务和角色分配。

15.3.3 Automation Use Principle

15.3.3 自动化的使用原则

Both crew members should not deal with the FMS as the same time; one head up at all times!

两名机组人员不应同时操作飞行管理系统;两个飞行员不能同时低头,必须有一位飞行员抬起头来,目视前方!

(1) Automated equipment tends to increase hypo-vigilance.

(2) Programming is time consuming.

(3) Programming is a source of error. All programming actions must be crosschecked.

(4) The computers may fail: automated systems behavior must be monitored and crosschecked with raw data.

(1) 自动化设备往往会使飞行员警惕性低下。

(2) 执行新数据很耗时。

(3) 修改数据是错误的来源。每一步的输入都必须进行交叉检查。

(4) 计算机可能出现故障:必须对自动化进行监控,并与原始数据进行交叉核对。

References
参 考 文 献

[1] 罗晓利．飞行中的人的因素 [M]. 3 版. 成都：西南交通大学出版社，2017.
[2] 徐宝纲，等．机组资源管理 [M]. 北京：清华大学出版社，2012.
[3] 罗晓利．机组资源管理 [M]. 成都：西南交通大学出版社，2002.
[4] Robert L Helmreich . Crew Resource Management [M]. 2nd Edition. ACDEMIC PRESS，2010.
[5] Laurentiu Dumitras. The evolution of crew resource management [C]. The 8th International Scientific Conference "DEFENSE RESOURCES MANAGEMENT IN THE 21st CENTURY" Braşov，November 14th，2013.
[6] Rene Amalberti，et al. Briefings a human factors course for pilots and aviation professionals [M]. Dedale S. A，2000.
[7] Federal Aviation Administration. Pilot's Handbook of Aeronautical Knowledge [M]. Aviation Supplies & Academics Inc，2009.
[8] 尚立琴，杨虎，汪磊. 国际航班飞行员复诵差错影响因素研究 [J]. 安全与环境学报，2021，1(8)：1-3.